PRAISE FOR
IN A RELATIONSHIP WITH GOD

"Your relationship with God, how is it?"

To provide an adequate response to this seemingly casual question, Zelda, one of our Master of Christian Studies graduates in 2017, endeavors to integrate the four fundamental doctrines of creation, soteriology, ecclesiology, and eschatology, while attempting to make them relevant and applicable in the daily contexts of a Christian disciple. She manages to articulate the quintessence of her subtle reflections in a clear and succinct manner. I had the honor and privilege of reading through an early draft of her manuscript back in August 2020, and am thankful and excited indeed to see it getting published now in 2023, in both Chinese and English for a readership worldwide.

This book is perhaps not to be taken as an academic monograph, though its arguments encompass the many critical discourses going on in biblical and theological classes. There may not be moving testimonies or 'chicken soup for the soul' type of stories to tug at your heartstrings; the sincere and candid style of writing, however, is evident of a conscientious personal confession emerging from the depth of one's heart and mind, to be received and treasured with the same level of earnestness.

The relationship between God and humanity has always been complex enough to defy any water-tight rational or logical propositions. No wonder Harold Bloom (*The Book of J* Random House 1990), a contemporary Jewish literary critic, raises the pertinent question to everybody's surprise: Could the Pentateuchal document 'J' three millennia ago be authored by a most intelligent and perceptive princess belonging to the house of David in Jerusalem?

— **Rev. Prof. Stephen Lee**
President Emeritus
China Graduate School of Theology, Hong Kong

"'Relationship' can be such a trendy term that is often devoid of any significant value, but this volume rehabilitates such a concept by providing a firm foundation upon which a meaningful invitation to walk with God can be issued. Through the lens of "relationship," Cheung provides a helpful entry point into navigating the tension between faith and works, the effects of the Fall and the present experience of the new life, as well as the importance of an individual's personal response to divine grace and the living out of one's faith within one's community. It is not a volume to be devoured in one sitting; instead, it serves as a dialogue partner that provides both guidance and encouragement for those who are to experience the power of the gospel afresh in their journey of faith."

— **Rev. Prof. David W. Pao**
Academic Dean & Professor of New Testament
Trinity Evangelical Divinity School

"It is an honor to witness the evolution of this volume from its preliminary phase to the published systematic teaching material that it is today. In this book, Cheung responds to a most critical question: the core of a life transformed by the gospel is not a list of religious activities; instead, it is reclaiming the focus on "relationship" as a foundational element in our faith. Through various bible passages, Cheung guides the readers to rediscover the importance of "relationship," revealing how it permeates commonly used religious terms such as "gospel," "the Fall of mankind," "the church," etc. This book is written for any believer who wants to renew and rekindle their faith, as it is written without religious jargon that could feel dry and hollow, nor does it linger on theological discussions that are difficult to digest. Combining an accessible writing style with a solid theological foundation, this book gently guides its readers on a journey of life renewal."

— **Rev. Dr. Simon Cheung**
Dean & Henry Co See Cho Associate Professor (Biblical Studies)
China Graduate School of Theology, Hong Kong

"Reading this book is like going through a spiritual journey of faith. It helps us understand our relationship with God, the necessity of our walk with Him, and how we let God be the center of our relationships with others. The reflection questions in each chapter encourage us to meditate and look honestly into our state of spiritual life. This book integrates exegesis, theology, and spirituality skillfully in an accessible language."

— **Rev. Dr. Philip Chan**
Senior Pastor
Hong Kong Baptist Church

Reader Testimonials

"Having been a believer for years, I have always thought that I have some understanding of certain core Christian concepts. But on reading this book, it is like God is by my side to remind me once again why I need to believe in Him and why the gift of salvation that came through Jesus's sacrifice is so precious. He has re-inspired me to understand the true meaning of trusting in Him continually. This book has also prompted me to re-examine and reflect on my relationship with God. Through this book, God reminds me that in this chaotic world, I should not rely on my own will to steer my life. Instead, I need to rely on Him at all times and learn to fellowship with Him through daily devotion and payers, so that I will know how to follow His will and serve Him, and build a more intimate relationship with Him. This book is rich and concise. The reflection questions in each chapter encourage in-depth reflection on different aspects of our relationship with God, which is highly beneficial for both new converts and those who have been believers for a while. I praise the Lord for using Zelda so we can experience how remarkable it is to walk with God through this book."

— **Mr. Tom Tong**

"This is a book about the most important relationship in our lives. Like any other relationship, we are reminded that our relationship with God is reciprocal—there is a call and a response—and it is alive. As the author points out time after time, every day we can make the decision to share our moments of joy, desire, difficulty, fear, sadness, and exhaustion with God, looking to Him as our most intimate companion, loving provider, righteous guide, and powerful Saviour. Or, we can choose to live in our own little orbit, where we already decide what is best for us and whom to reach out to whenever we experience life's ups and downs. Many of us invest in our relationships with significant others, family and friends, people at church, and in the workplace. Yet, are we making nearly as much effort to be in a functional and loving relationship with God each day? When we spend our days without relating to God, we are effectively declaring that we are not in a relationship with God without even realising it. This book makes us take a new look at the meaning of being in a relationship with God and confront the current state of this single most important aspect of our lives. By helping us grasp the true nature of God's love and salvation through a series of reflections, the author also guides us to revisit our walk with God, reminding us of the important notion of "relationship before works," extending it to the church community, and asking us to examine our priorities in life with an awareness that time is limited. Using easy-to-understand language and logic, the author convinces us to take action today to renew our faith in God and declare our love for Him."

— **Dr. Anna Wong**

IN A RELATIONSHIP WITH GOD

IN A RELATIONSHIP WITH GOD

MAKING SENSE OF YOUR CHRISTIAN FAITH

ZELDA CHEUNG

IN A RELATIONSHIP WITH GOD
Copyright © 2023 Zelda Cheung
All rights reserved.

Published 2023 by AIME Publishing
Vancouver, British Columbia
www.aimepublishing.com

ISBN: 978-1-7380011-0-1

All Scripture quotations, unless otherwise indicated, are taken from the Holy Bible, New International Version®, NIV®. Copyright ©1973, 1978, 1984, 2011 by Biblica, Inc.® Used by permission of Zondervan. All rights reserved worldwide. www.zondervan.com The "NIV" and "New International Version" are trademarks registered in the United States Patent and Trademark Office by Biblica, Inc.®

Scripture quotations marked (ESV) are from The ESV® Bible (The Holy Bible, English Standard Version®), copyright © 2001 by Crossway, a publishing ministry of Good News Publishers. Used by permission. All rights reserved.

Scripture quotations marked (NASB) are from the (NASB®) New American Standard Bible®, Copyright © 1960, 1971, 1977, 1995, 2020 by The Lockman Foundation. Used by permission. All rights reserved. www.lockman.org

No portion of this book may be reproduced in any form without written permission from the publisher or author, except as permitted by copyright law.

CONTENTS

Preface	xiii
How is Your Relationship with God?	xvii
1. Revisiting the Good News	1

I. UNDERSTANDING OUR RELATIONSHIP WITH GOD

2. God's Original Design	21
3. Broken by Sin	33
4. Revelation through Jesus	44
5. Application: Walking with God	55
Special topic: The Love and Justice of God	77

II. A COMMUNITY OF GOD'S CHILDREN

6. There Is Only One Community	89
7. Application: Living as One Community	101
8. The Bride Awaiting Her Groom	124
9. Application: Keeping the End in Mind	142
Special Topic: Predestination	152
Conclusion: Leaning on God as His Beloved	158
References	167
Notes	169

Here I am! I stand at the door and knock.
If anyone hears my voice and opens the door,
I will come in and eat with that person, and they with me.

Revelation 3:20

PREFACE

Writing a book was the last thing on my mind. I knew it would be long and arduous, and possibly a complete waste of effort. I did not feel qualified, and I was doubtful if I would have anything to share that is not already better enunciated by others more knowledgeable and insightful than I. Thus, in my prayers, I had always asked, "Why?" Yet God knows things we have forgotten, and works in ways we do not understand. Right when I needed to put together a preface, I randomly stumbled upon a file on my computer that documents the spark that, I now realize, was the beginning of this entire journey:

> I have noticed for a while now that I am burned out in my attempt to serve God. I have strived to be faithful in my service, but I find myself seeking more. In fact, I have been bending myself over to be more faithful. But, then, for what? Is it to finally get someone to acknowledge that I am faithful? Is it to show God that I am faithful? Or is this just what God's people do, serving faithfully? I realize I am at a loss for words.

PREFACE

Frankly, I do not doubt that we, as followers of Christ, are to serve faithfully. That is certainly true, and that is exactly what I've strived to do all these years. But if that is the case, then how do I walk away feeling hollow and even less intimate with God?

I try to reconcile my exhaustion with the fact that God created me, loves me, and freely gave Jesus's life for my sins—and I cannot help but notice that underneath that faithful façade, something is amiss. Honesty is missing. A growing relationship is missing. My only way of interacting with God has become the model of a bad marriage. I try to keep my end of our agreement, but there is so little joy and intimacy. I am weary, but I am not to tell God. I sometimes hate the situations I am in, but I am not to tell God.

The truth is, I don't even dare to tell myself. Because when I do, when I see the truth for what it really is, I feel that I would not have the momentum to keep going. My exhaustion will take over, and I will finally look like the unfaithful person I fear that I am. The one who stops serving, who fails to persevere for God. But what happened to delighting in the Lord? Could I say I have delighted in the Lord when all I do is serve without truly cherishing our relationship, without enjoying His presence? And I know right there that there is a problem. Maybe others don't share my problem. Maybe others have kept up with their impeccable service and still managed to nurture an intimate relationship with God.

But I haven't.

My service has given me the false impression that I am doing so well in my faith. But I have spent all my time fulfilling these duties while skimming on my personal time with God. I have prayed with everyone else, but rarely alone. I have learned scripture from sermons and hymns, but not in my private time with God. In fact, I am having less and less private time with God, because I am so out of time. Between work and family and time spent at church, I

PREFACE

am not more energized, because I am often just drained. Should I continue to lie to myself that I am not tired, when I really am, and God knows full well that I am? Is this the only way I can be faithful? What does being faithful in my walk with God really mean?

My own struggles and exhaustion became the very impetus for my exploration, as I wrestled with what it means to walk with God and have a good relationship with Him. I certainly was not planning to write a book on the topic, but that was the beginning, the seed God planted. What followed was months of reflection and prayers, as I read and studied His words, revisiting what I learned in seminary, and practiced dialoguing and walking with Him through the daily grind of this daunting journey of writing. He showed me, literally, what it is like to be with Him, to have Him as my guide and mentor, my comforter, my Lord, every step of the way. This end product is God's answer to my questions, a testament to His faithfulness, love, and grace.

So if you are still reading, I hope this book will help you the way it helped me, if God permits. May this be a blessing in your quest to know and love God and walk with Him the way He wants us to.

HOW IS YOUR RELATIONSHIP WITH GOD?

The answer to this question is not necessarily straightforward. Some might say with confidence that their relationship with God is good. Others would admit that the relationship is mediocre, distant, or non-existent. Still, some are unsure of how to answer this question, because having a relationship with God is a concept that can be vague and elusive. As Christians, we are likely aware that our relationship with God is important, yet we never quite know what it entails and how to define it. Many of us strive to have a good relationship with God by doing what we were told since the days of our conversion: we pray, we go to church, we read the Bible, we take part in ministry, and we preach the gospel. But is that all there is to having a relationship with God? Is our relationship with God measured merely by how well we check items off this list? Are we supposed to feel warm, loved, and intimate in our relationship with Him, or is it about faithfulness and obedience?

These questions reveal that for many of us, the understanding of what it means to have a relationship with God is far from complete. Regardless of how long we have been Christians, we could still be searching for a clearer understanding and a better definition to help us make sense of our faith. After all, the journey of following Christ is full of ups and downs, replete with its share of challenges and struggles—challenges that are only heightened by our rapidly changing world. We seemingly know a lot about God, His love, His grace, and the ways we are supposed to live as followers of Christ, but we are much less sure of how to apply this knowledge to our lives. It is disorienting when teachings in the Bible feel disconnected and irrelevant to the hurdles we face in this increasingly confusing world. We might be eager to live a life pleasing to God, a life characterized by the joy and peace promised time and again in the Bible. Yet what we often experience are doubt and exhaustion in our attempt to walk faithfully with Him.

Is that how you feel as well, sometimes? The good news is: our God is faithful, even when we are doubtful and confused. God never leaves us alone to figure out how to walk with Him, because "His divine power has given us *everything* we need for a godly life through the knowledge of Him who called us by His own glory and goodness" (2 Pet. 1:3). In fact, while we might have looked at our relationship with God as an ambiguous entity that is simply there because we are saved, the relationship is so much more than a list of activities to be completed, or something for us to excel at. As we reexamine and expand on what we know about our relationship with God, we will see that it is the very *means* that will give us the strength and knowledge we need to navigate our faith in our daily circumstances. It is the context that will enable us to piece together our fragmented knowledge of God, ourselves, and our faith into a coherent framework—one through which we learn to truly abide in Him and live the life God has promised for His children. If you have been struggling in your walk with God, or you simply yearn to grow deeper in your relationship with Him, I invite you to embark on this journey of reflection and transformation, so that we can live out our calling as God's faithful witnesses in today's world.

HOW IS YOUR RELATIONSHIP WITH GOD?

How to use this book—make this your personal journey of reflection and growth

We live in a time of endless information and knowledge. In fact, you might have picked up this book because you feel that it contains new insights for growing deeper in your walk with God. Nonetheless, to make this book your personal journey of reflection and reevaluation, I invite you to take an additional step and proactively engage with the material presented here. At the beginning of each chapter, there will be questions to help you reflect on the current state of your spiritual life, or your understanding of various theological concepts. I encourage you to get a journal or a notebook and set aside time for quietness and prayerful introspection as you go through each chapter. Pray and spend some time thinking about your personal view regarding these questions, and write down your honest reflections and responses in your journal. At the end of each chapter, there will be further questions or summary points for you to see how your understanding may have evolved through the chapter. By including these reflection questions in the chapters, I hope this will be an opportunity for you to think deeply, at your own pace, about these concepts and your relationship with God, without worrying about sounding wrong or unspiritual. Let us develop the habit of looking inward and giving ourselves the space to honestly examine our hearts and our understanding, because this is where we will meet God and be healed, shaped, and transformed. May this journey of reflection be the very exercise for you to experience God and His unfathomable goodness in your walk with Him.

1. REVISITING THE GOOD NEWS
WHAT WE MAY HAVE FORGOTTEN OR NEVER QUITE UNDERSTOOD

It might be a little unexpected that our journey to redefining our relationship with God begins with the basics—the gospel. Indeed, for those of us who have been believers for a while, the good news may feel like a dubious starting point because we already know it so well! We have all heard it (and possibly preached it) countless times: we are sinners who are saved because we accepted the gift of salvation through faith, a gift made available through the sacrifice of Jesus Christ on the cross. Nonetheless, what we are often oblivious to is how much of what we know about our relationship with God comes from our understanding of the good news. Not only did we first become aware of our relationship with God when the gospel was preached to us, but inherent in the good news are concepts like sin, judgment, righteousness, and faith. These concepts are complex and possibly difficult for us to fully grasp when we were new converts, but they are crucial in our walk with God. Therefore, before we reconstruct our understanding of how we should relate to God, let us return to several key elements in the gospel, and refresh our understanding of facets of the good news that we may have forgotten, or never quite understood.

Reflection Question

1. What is salvation according to your understanding? Is it to gain eternal life and, therefore, entry into heaven? Is it a lifestyle change? Is it learning about God and having a relationship with Him? Or is it all of the above?

Key Concept #1: Why do we need salvation?
Because we are sinners who will face judgment when Jesus comes back at the end time.

"WE ARE SINNERS" is a hard truth that keeps many non-believers from accepting the gospel. In today's world, where good and bad are seen as relative, any mention of sin is found to be offensive by many. Yet this is a question that cannot be avoided in any presentation of the good news. But what does it mean to be a sinner? How are we sinners? Rom. 3:23 tells us that "for all have sinned and fall short of the glory of God"; not only that, but "the wages of sin is death" (Rom. 6:23). These verses remind us of several important truths. First, they remind us that there is a standard, a way for human beings to *be* during our time on earth, and this standard is *defined by God*. God is watching every thought and every action, and will one day judge each of us in accordance with how we have lived based on this standard. Second, when we fail to meet this standard, there are consequences—and the price to pay for living in a sinful way is death. Third, none of us can reach God's standard with our own effort because *all* have sinned. Therefore the sad and inevitable endpoint for everybody is death.

But what is this "death" that the scripture is referring to? The

1. REVISITING THE GOOD NEWS

second half of Rom. 6:23 provides the much-needed clarification: "for the wages of sin is death, *but the gift of God is eternal life in Christ Jesus our Lord.*" The opposite of death is having eternal life, which is the life granted to those deemed righteous when God brings judgment on everyone. Therefore, on the one hand, this death refers to the eternal death that comes when one fails to meet God's standard on the day of judgment. It signifies eternal separation from God when everything on earth passes away, and is replaced by the new heaven and new earth described in the book of Revelation.

On the other hand, since death is associated with separation from God, death also signifies a broken relationship with God. Indeed, even before the arrival of the day of judgment, our relationship with God is already broken as sinners. One expression of this broken relationship is depicted as God "giving us over" to our sinful desires to do what ought not to be done (Rom. 1:24–31). Sin blocks our way to God because He is holy. As sinners, we are God's enemies and are hostile toward Him. Apart from God, we continue in our sinful ways, and our perpetual inability to live up to God's standard paves the way to the eternal death that inevitably awaits us upon Jesus's return. In Paul's words, this is equivalent to "storing up wrath against yourself for the day of God's wrath, when His righteous judgment will be revealed" (Rom. 2:5).

In summary, there are five takeaways from the first key concept of the good news:

- God defines the standard of righteous living.
- God will judge everyone upon Jesus's return based on how we have lived.
- For those who fail to meet God's standard of righteous living, the consequence is death.
- Only those deemed righteous during the final judgment can avoid this death and be granted eternal life, but this is a standard nobody can meet.
- Death signifies a broken relationship with God and the eventual eternal separation from God. Thus the hostility

between God and us has significance both in our current lives and in the end time.

The picture presented in the Bible reveals that God holds absolute authority in this world and our existence as the Creator and Lord of all creation. He alone defines right and wrong, and He alone has the authority to judge and grant eternal life. It also reminds us that our relationship with God does not exist only when we accept Christ. It has always been there, but it is broken by sins, leaving us utterly oblivious to God and our relationship with Him before our conversion. Sadly, for many of us, the longer we have been believers, the less we think about sin, judgment, and the end time. We have grown increasingly callous about the impact of sins in our lives, and have a far diminished awareness of the impending end. We forget that God's judgment will come upon us, believers and non-believers alike, based on every action and thought during our time on earth (Rev. 20:12; 2 Cor. 5:10). Jesus will return like a thief, at an hour that no one knows, and we need to be ready (Matt. 24:44). Yet often we are so focused on the here and now that we lose sight of eternity, not realizing that this awareness of the end time is critical in informing the way we relate to God and others now. We will return to this important concept later in the book.

Points for Reflection

1. If we believe that God is the Creator and thus has every authority to establish the rules of this world, then what constitutes sins is not defined by us or our societies, but in accordance with His sovereignty. What does this mean for you, and how does this make you feel? Write down your reflection in your journal; pray and ask God to help you comprehend its significance and implications, and to

1. REVISITING THE GOOD NEWS

    remember His love and goodness if you are unnerved by His sovereignty.
2. Sins lead to broken relationships with God. Do you see how this broken relationship and this sense of alienation is displayed in your life (before your conversion or now) and the lives of those around you?

_____

Key Concept #2: What is God's plan of salvation for us?
God the Father sent His only begotten son Jesus Christ, who is sinless, to die on the cross for our sins and was subsequently raised from the dead to make salvation available to all.

IF ALL HAVE SINNED and fall short of the glory of God, how does anyone stand a chance? If we let our minds stay on the previous section, it is so easy to think of God as the merciless judgmental God who is only out to put people to death. But John 3:16 tells us that *"for God so loved the world* that He gave His one and only Son, that whoever believes in Him shall not perish but have eternal life." God does not want us to perish. He is not some sadistic God who cannot wait for us to die a second death because of our sins. Rather, in His love, He has prepared a way out for all sinners, a pathway to eternal life, because God knows that humans in our sinful nature will never be able to live up to His standard of righteous living. In fact, the single most powerful proof of God's love is the way He chose to make salvation available to all while we were still constantly triggering His wrath with our sins. Rom. 5:8 says, "But God demonstrates His own love for us in this: While we were still sinners, Christ died for us."

God is love (1 John 4:8), even in the face of our sins. In His love, God has chosen to *credit us* with His righteousness as a gift, opening the door to salvation by God's own work and plan through the death and resurrection of Jesus Christ. It is thus a gift that only becomes available on God's initiative. In addition, it is a gift that is extremely costly and precious because Jesus, who is God and sinless, not only became fully human but also died the most excruciating death so that *everyone* who accepts this gift can be called righteous. It is in this sense that the gift is unconditional, because the right to receive this gift is not dependent on who we are and what we do. It is a gift that cannot be earned, but freely given. This is how much God loves us.

Why did Jesus have to die?

Yet have you ever wondered why did Jesus have to die? If God is the Creator who made all the rules, why can't God just wipe away all our sins? This is because God is still the same just and righteous God who will judge us at the end time. The wages of sin is still death, and *someone* will still need to pay for the unrighteousness committed. So often, we have a hard time understanding God's way because we do not always see the importance of justice. But all it takes is a simple scenario to illustrate why it is crucial. Imagine if you had been wronged, and God waved it off and said, "It's all good!" Wouldn't you be outraged by the injustice of it all, wondering if God indeed loves you if He allows such hurtful acts to go unpunished? We want God to be loving and forgiving when we are the perpetrator, but we want Him to be just when we are the victims. Yet in actuality, all of us are *both* perpetrators and victims in this fallen world, and we realize that it is neither just nor loving to simply dismiss everyone's sins.

This example shows us a glimpse of why a price must be paid for our sins. It also reveals that God's way of bringing salvation is, in fact, a manifestation of both His love and justice. Seeing that we cannot bear the cost of our sins, God bore the price by sending His only son as a sacrifice of atonement to pay the wages of both past and future sins of mankind, once and for all (Rom. 3:25). Through Jesus's blood we can be justified and considered as righteous during the final judgment, evading the just outcome for sinners at the end time—eternal death. In God's grace, we will get to live in eternity

1. REVISITING THE GOOD NEWS

with God, witnessing the new creation and the inauguration of God's full eternal reign. This is the first aspect of God's plan of salvation for us.

But there is more to being saved. Not only did Jesus Christ die on the cross for us, but He was raised from the dead on the third day, demonstrating that death and sins no longer have mastery over Him (Rom. 6:9). Our God is a victorious God who through Jesus's sacrifice released humanity from the complete grip of sin, thereby relieving us from the inevitable agony and suffering brought on by a fallen world. This is the second aspect of salvation. Our relationship with God is put right once again, so that through abiding in Jesus, it is now *possible* to live a life pleasing to God while we are still on earth.

In fact, this restored relationship is at the center of the salvation offered to us. In Jesus's prayer to God the Father, He said, "Now this is eternal life: that they *know* you, the only true God, and Jesus Christ, whom You have sent" (John 17:3). Through the restoration of our relationship with God, we will *know* God. We will learn to follow Him and fellowship with Him as His children and heirs, eventually sharing in the future glory of new creation when Jesus returns. "Those who are victorious will inherit all this, and I will be their God and they will be my children" (Rev. 21:7). What is achieved through Jesus's costly sacrifice is thus a complete salvation that not only saves us from eternal death at the final judgment, but also reconciles us to God, thereby setting us on a path of new life on earth that eventually prepares us for eternal fellowship with God.

Below are the reminders that emerged from our discussion of the gospel's second key concept:

- Salvation comes only from the love of God. Death being the fate of sinners is a just outcome; God only provides a way out because He loves us.
- Salvation is made available entirely on God's initiative.
- Jesus had to die because God is righteous.

- Jesus's blood paid the price of our sins so that those who accept this gift can be credited as righteous during the final judgment.
- Jesus's sacrifice and resurrection enabled reconciliation and restoration of mankind's relationship with God, so that those who accept this gift can be released from the bondage of sin and live a life pleasing to God.

Regarding salvation, it is interesting to observe two disparate mentalities among believers. Some think of salvation primarily as a ticket to heaven, as salvation from eternal damnation in the future, so how we live today matters little. Others are so engrossed in our daily routines as believers that we forget that we are sojourners, that eternal life is about life *after* the end when we will fellowship with God in eternity. Yet God's word reminds us that salvation is both. It is rescuing us from eternal death during the final judgment, as well as deliverance from the bondage of sin while we are still here. The restoration of our relationship with God is not a side benefit, but the very blessing of salvation through which we can abide in Him daily, starting with our time on earth and extending into eternity.

An equally important reminder is that God's plan of salvation allows us to witness the simultaneous display of God's justice and love, qualities we believe are polar opposites and thus irreconcilable. So often, we think that because Jesus has already died on the cross for us, our sins have lost their vileness, and God is no longer offended. Yet God is too just and holy to overlook the sins we still commit every day, but also too loving to let us pay the price on our own. Coming to grips with this tension grants us a newfound awe of God's love and grace and a deeper appreciation of Jesus's costly sacrifice. We see the weight Jesus had to bear for our sins and how much we still need the blood of Jesus to cover our sins daily. God's ways are indeed not our ways, for His ways are higher, wiser, albeit sometimes unfathomable to us. Yet this is the beginning of us learning to see Him not as whom we want Him to be, but *knowing* Him as who He really is. This is the journey we will continue in subsequent chapters, as our understanding of God, of ourselves,

1. REVISITING THE GOOD NEWS

and what it means to have a relationship with Him is refined and realigned.

Points for Reflection

1. Salvation is not simply the granting of eternal life when Jesus returns at the end time. It is the restoration of our relationship with God so we can be saved from sins *today*. How does this realization affect the way you look at your weaknesses and the struggles you face each day?
2. God's plan of salvation demonstrates both His love and justice—the justice to not let any sins go unpunished and the love to pay the price on our behalf by sending Jesus Christ for us. Does this change your understanding of God and the salvation He offers?

Key Concept #3: How do we receive this gift of salvation? How are our lives different as believers?

The gift of salvation can only be received through faith in Jesus Christ. Believers are to live a life led by the Holy Spirit, who dwells in those who genuinely belong to God.

FOR A GIFT that grants salvation from the bondage of sin and eternal damnation, there is probably nothing more important than knowing how to receive this gift. One might wonder why this step is necessary since Jesus's sacrifice has made salvation available to all. But there is an unmistakably *personal* component to salvation. The relationship that is restored is our personal relationship with God, and eternal life is given only to those who accept this gift. Receiving this gift is thus a personal choice, a conscious decision made with our God-given free will when we choose to place our faith in Jesus Christ. Rom. 10:10 gives us a clear formula for accepting this gift. "For it is with your heart that you believe and are justified, and it is with your mouth that you profess your faith and are saved." Salvation is thus a gift to be received by faith in Jesus Christ when we believe in Him and declare our choice to believe in Him.

What does it mean to have faith?

But if someone were to ask, "What does it mean to have faith in Jesus?" or "What *exactly* are we to believe to receive the gift of salvation?" We will probably state the obvious—it is believing that Jesus Christ is our Savior. Indeed, faith in Jesus is believing what the gospel tells us about God and ourselves. It is believing that we are sinners who need salvation. It is believing that Jesus is indeed God who became fully human, who died on the cross, and was raised on the third day to pay for our personal sins. It is putting our faith in Jesus, trusting that His blood will cover our transgressions and bring eternal life at the time of final judgment. It is believing that salvation restores our relationship with God the moment we receive this gift, thereby replacing the hostility that once stood between God and us with peace.

But since the word "faith" in Greek also means "trust and reliance,"[1] having faith also signifies *continual* reliance on God and the *continual* choice to believe in Jesus Christ. Being saved through faith is, therefore, not the temporary adoption of a set of beliefs, but a persistent change in mindset and allegiance. Instead of relying on ourselves to be good people and somehow secure salvation on our own, we continually trust that in God's faithfulness, He will ensure that our pledge of allegiance will still be considered legitimate at the end time. The restored, ongoing relationship with God is manifested as us repenting (i.e., turning away) from self-reliance and our old way of life, and returning to God by trusting Him as our Lord and Savior. We are no longer our own master; we belong to God, and the Holy Spirit dwells in us (Rom. 8:9). We have been given a new identity as a member of God's kingdom, saved to become part of God's Church, the body of Christ.

With a new allegiance comes a new way of life. The Holy Spirit now intercedes for us to help us live in a way that pleases God, so that we can be released from the bondage of sin and grow to be more like Christ. It is a lifelong process that requires our continual reliance on Christ. This is what Paul means with the repeated use of the phrase "in Christ" to describe this restored relationship with God (Rom. 8:1; 1 Cor. 1:30; 2 Cor. 5:17; Gal. 3:26): we are redeemed *in Christ*; we are justified *in Christ*; we will receive eternal life *in Christ*. Jesus said, "I am the vine; you are the branches. If you remain in Me and I in you, you will bear much fruit; apart from Me you can do nothing" (John 15:5). We only bear fruit if we stay *in Christ*, and when Jesus returns, we too will share in God's glory as His children and heirs.

Salvation by faith or by work?

Yet once the notion of bearing fruit enters the picture, it brings new confusion regarding salvation. Eph. 2:8–9 says, "For it is by grace you have been saved, through faith—and this is not from yourselves, it is the gift of God—not by works, so that no one can boast." The scripture clearly distinguishes between the contribution of faith and work in our salvation, emphatically reminding us that salvation is neither from ourselves nor by work, but it is a gift of God's grace that can only be accepted through faith. Yet James 2:17 (ESV) states that "faith by itself, if it does not have works (or deeds or actions)[2], is dead." These verses have left many unsure of how to interpret the interrelation of faith and work in our salvation and daily life as Christians, resulting in many questions. For example, what is work? Does our conscious decision to accept the gift of salvation count as being "from ourselves"? If our faith is dead in the absence of work, what is the relationship between salvation and bearing fruit?

To answer these questions, we need to reexamine our understanding of "gift" and "work." So often, because we are told that salvation is an unconditional gift given freely to us, we take it to mean that we have no responsibility whatsoever regarding God's invitation, and all that is required of us is passive concurrence. But when we understand salvation as the restoration of our relationship with God, we will see we do have our share of responsibility in this relationship. God might have taken the initiative to prepare this wonderful gift in His grace, but we have the responsibility to *respond*. Us choosing to accept this gift through faith is thus not only our personal and active response to God's call, but it is a decision that takes commitment—the commitment to continually honor God as our Savior and Lord, placing our faith in Him and relying on Him. In this sense, salvation is more than a transaction, but a relationship, a covenant that requires our continual commitment.

The intention to remain committed to this restored relationship is precisely what Jesus described with the analogy of the vine and branches (John 15:1–8). We are urged to remain in Him, and He will remain in us, because when we continue to abide in Jesus, fruit will come forth through the grace of God. It is a natural outcome when we are in Christ, when we, the branches, are joined to the vine. Our transformed life and good deeds/works will then be the very evidence of our restored relationship and our new identity in Christ. After all, we are *supposed to be different* in our deeds as redeemed sinners because the Holy Spirit lives in us. This is what James is referring to when he said, "Faith without works is dead," because if we have stayed in Christ through faith in Jesus, actions (i.e., good works) should result to reflect our faith. On the other hand, if no actions are springing forth, then one has to wonder if this person was genuinely reconciled to God in the first place.

The discussion above shows that even though salvation is a gift, good works and us living in a way that pleases God are still important in our lives as saved sinners. Therefore, when Paul states that salvation is not by works, it is not to say that good works are optional in Christian living, but it is to remind us that we have done *nothing* to earn the gift of salvation. Work is not *how* we obtain salvation, nor how branches are joined to the vine. Rather, good work is what happens *after* we are saved, because fruit comes only

1. REVISITING THE GOOD NEWS

after the branches are joined to the vine, not before. It reminds us that regardless of how righteous we think we are, no one can reach God's standard to gain eligibility for salvation or achieve salvation on our own. Nor can we do good works that glorify God or make fruit grow with our own effort, because apart from God, we can do nothing. We can only remain in Him and witness God's grace at work.

This is why Eph. 2:8–9 ends with "so that no one can boast." It warns us against an attitude of pride and self-reliance, of feeling like we can earn or secure salvation through our effort. We must not look at salvation like the wage and salary we earn and are entitled to due to our hard work, because if something is considered a wage or salary, it is no longer a gift. Thus when Paul reminds us that salvation is a gift, it is to urge us to look at salvation with a grateful heart, so that *we will not take credit for what God has achieved*. Indeed, the Bible tells us that even those who made the decision to accept Christ were prompted by God. Jesus said, "No one can come to Me unless the Father who sent Me draws them" (John 6:44). God has always been the one who opens our eyes to our need for salvation, and the one who calls us in the first place. We have nothing to boast about, because salvation is a pure gift, and God's grace precedes our responses or actions. This is an important truth we must not lose sight of.

The third key concept of the gospel gives us several essential reminders:

- The gift of salvation is to be accepted through faith in Jesus Christ alone. None of us can work to earn salvation.
- Accepting the gift of salvation is a conscious decision made on our part, a commitment of continual faith in Jesus Christ.
- Accepting the gift of salvation is a restoration of our relationship with God, a switch in allegiance and mindset from self-reliance to God-reliance.

- Our faith and restored relationship with God should be reflected in good works that result from us abiding in Jesus.

When we are reminded of the new, Spirit-led life that God blesses His children with, or how fruit-bearing should happen naturally and seemingly effortlessly, sometimes it leaves us confused and dejected because it is such a far cry from our daily reality. Indeed, despite all our knowledge about God and salvation, living out the Bible's teaching continues to be a challenge. We want to live a life pleasing to God, yet we struggle. We want to place our faith in Him instead of relying on ourselves, but we falter. Paul captures the struggle we all face candidly in Rom. 7:19–20, "For I know that good itself does not dwell in me, that is, in my sinful nature. For I have the desire to do what is good, but I cannot carry it out. For I do not do the good I want to do, but the evil I do not want to do—this I keep on doing." The battle is real and inevitable, especially when we do try to follow the Holy Spirit. Each day we are tempted to follow our old way of life because we are in a fallen world where our old self and sinful nature are very much still with us. We are used to being the master instead of choosing to honor God as Lord.

Then what are we to do? Does it mean that we will only be trapped in the never-ending cycle of struggle and frustration until the final victory is won with Jesus's return? This is when we must remember to look to Jesus, the pioneer and perfecter of our faith (Heb. 12:2). God never intends for us to fight the battle alone. In fact, He has already given us the very weapon we need to overcome the bondage of sin during our time on earth—our restored relationship with Him. We are branches that have already been joined to the vine through the blood of Jesus. As we learn to abide in Jesus and become more familiar with the voice of the Holy Spirit, we will learn to draw on the grace and strength of God to choose to follow God instead. We will come to enjoy the peace and gratitude that fill our hearts, knowing that every good work will be accomplished through His strength, not ours.

In the upcoming chapters, we will deepen and widen our

understanding of how we should relate to God and what it means to remain in Him. We will also discuss how our personal relationship with God integrates with our identity as a member of God's community. As we continue to seek God with humility and an open mind, we can trust that God will speak to us and help us learn to truly follow Him. We can count on this because Jesus Himself has declared that He is our good shepherd (John 10:11). He who grants us the incomparable gift of salvation will watch over us and teach us, because He loves us so very much.

Points for Reflection

1. The discussion above reminds us that salvation is through faith alone and not to be earned by works. However, sometimes we might still be trying to earn our salvation because we feel unworthy of the gift. Have you had this experience? Do you sometimes catch yourself still trying to prove that you are worthy of this gift?
2. Salvation is continual faith in Jesus and a shift from relying on ourselves to relying on God. What areas in your life have you learned to rely on God instead of yourself? What is something that may make it difficult for you to trust God?

Part I
Understanding Our Relationship with God

Our review of the gospel reminds us that a restored relationship with God is at the center of our salvation. This perspective brings new insights into how we should interact with God as believers. First, it reminds us that salvation is not a one-off transaction where our interaction with God is done after we accept the gift of salvation. Rather, as a relationship, it signifies ongoing interaction and fellowship with God. Second, a relationship is never stagnant. It changes and evolves, for the better or worse. Our relationship with God is, therefore, something that needs to be nurtured. Third, similar to other relationships in our lives, the way we interact with God is determined by our understanding of the two parties in the relationship, i.e., God and ourselves. This understanding sets our expectations and determines the very nature and character of the relationship, which will then inform the way we interact in this relationship.

Therefore, to know how we should interact with God, we must first ask: who is God, and who are we in this restored relationship? These are questions we rarely ask ourselves, yet the Bible is full of passages that answer these questions. Specifically, the Bible contains multiple images to help us understand who God is, who we are, and how we should relate to Him. We are familiar with many of these images. For example, our God is the Creator, our Savior, our Lord, the shepherd—but notice how each of these imageries also reveals something about us. We are the sheep of our shepherd, the branches of the vine. We are saved sinners when we call Him our Savior, His children and heirs when we call Him our heavenly Father. Every new image adds to our knowledge of God and ourselves.

However, because some of these images are seemingly incompatible, we struggle to integrate these images into one coherent picture. Consequently, these images have remained as incongruent models in our heads, as we lean toward the ones that speak to us, while also shuffling between them based on our situations. Furthermore, not only are we each basing our relationship with God on different images, but our personal interpretations of these images differ. Unbeknownst to ourselves, we have often subconsciously drawn on our earthly models of various relationships to help us comprehend and visualize our relationship with God. This is a natural response because we are learning to relate to a God we cannot see. But it also means that our background and life experiences, ranging from our cultural and social background to the kind of familial relations we have, would all affect our interpretation of what it means to have a good relationship with God. Deeply hidden in our subconsciousness are our personal interpretations of the various images of God and ourselves, and it is this understanding that affects the way we interact with God daily.

This means that despite us all reading the same Bible and hearing similar teachings at church, we each have been interpreting our relationship with God slightly differently, and our understanding is, in fact, partial and personal. Therefore, to gain a more coherent and accurate picture of our relationship with God, we must first realign our understanding of God and ourselves with God's revelation. In this section, we will begin by returning to the Creation narrative in Genesis to look at God's original design of mankind's relationship with Him. We will then focus on the Fall of humanity in Genesis 3 to glean new insights into our current state and how sin ruined our relationship with God. Finally, we will learn from Jesus how we should relate to our heavenly Father.

2. GOD'S ORIGINAL DESIGN
WHAT THE CREATION NARRATIVE TEACHES US ABOUT OUR RELATIONSHIP WITH GOD

Reflection Questions

1. What is your perception of God? Do you think of Him as someone who is distant or stern? Or someone loving and warm?
2. How would you describe your relationship with God? How do you view yourself in this relationship with Him? Are you close to God or far from Him? Would you consider yourself a good child or the naughty one?

Since our relationship with God begins with our existence, let us return to the biblical accounts of the creation of mankind. It is a story we are all very familiar with. In Genesis 1, God created day and night, heaven and earth, land and sea, vegetation, the sun and the stars, evening and morning, and all sorts of living creatures. Then in Gen. 1:27, God decided to make mankind, male and female, in the image of God. And God made us with a specific purpose in mind. We are made so that we will "rule over the fish of the sea and over the birds of the sky and over the livestock and over all the earth, and over every crawling thing that crawls on the earth" (Gen. 1:26 NASB). Furthermore, in God's blessing, we are to "be fruitful and multiply, and fill the earth, and subdue it" (Gen. 1:28 NASB). Therefore, from the beginning, it is clear that we have our purpose, and our purpose is two-fold. First, we are to procreate and fill the earth. Second, we have a role in relation to the rest of creation, which is to have dominion over the earth and all living creatures.

But there is more. God knows the needs of mankind: He knows we need food, a place to stay, and things to do. So He said in Gen. 1:29, "I give you every seed-bearing plant on the face of the whole earth and every tree that has fruit with seed in it. They will be yours for food." God gave Adam, the first man created, a place to be when He planted a garden in Eden and placed Adam in the garden, asking him to "work it and take care of it" (Gen. 2:15). It was a garden that was well irrigated, where God made trees that were pleasing to the eyes and good for food to grow out of the ground (Gen. 2:9–10). Of course, in the middle of the garden were also the tree of life and the tree that would become the turning point of the entire story—the tree of the knowledge of good and evil. God commanded Adam that he could eat from any tree in the garden, except the tree of the knowledge of good and evil, because when he does, he will certainly die (Gen. 2:16–17). Knowing that "it is not good for the man to be alone," God brought all living creatures to Adam for him to name them, and to see if Adam could find a suitable helper. When none was found, God created a helper —a woman—to be with Adam (Gen. 2:18–20), and inaugurated the concept of marriage, where a man leaves his father and mother and is united to his wife and become one flesh (Gen. 2:24).

Such is the beauty of God's creation. God created the world as we know it: the stars, the sky, the ocean, the land, and every living

2. GOD'S ORIGINAL DESIGN

thing in this world. God created mankind, too, forming us from the dust of the earth. In the first two chapters of Genesis, God and His creation were in harmony and peace, with every party carrying out their roles according to God's perfect design. But within these two chapters are actually two accounts of Creation. If Chapter 1 is an account of Creation from a cosmic scale, then Chapter 2 specifically depicts how God made us, His prized creature, and how He looked after us on a personal level. Indeed, God's name changes from "God" in Gen. 1:1—2:3 to "the LORD God" in 2:4—3:24,[1] thus highlighting the intimate, personal relationship between the Creator and mankind.

In this second account of Creation, we see how man was given life when God breathed the breath of life into his nostril. God also handcrafted Adam's helper, the woman, from Adam's ribs after He put Adam in a deep sleep (Gen. 2:7; 2:21). We see God interacting with the first humans on a personal, intimate level in the Garden of Eden. They had direct access to God, readily dialoguing with God, and were continually in God's presence. As their Creator, God knew their every need, and He took the initiative to personally address their needs before they were even aware of them. He provided not only food, but food that was pleasing to the eyes. He gave instructions on what they should and should not do, and gave them purpose in their lives by giving them duties to carry out. God even provided a helper to ensure that Adam could carry out his duties to procreate and rule over creation, so that together they could experience the beauty of intimacy and fellowship in human relations. It is hard to imagine how the Creator who made the heaven and earth could also be so loving, personal, and intimate with us, His creature, but such is the picture depicted in the first two chapters of Genesis.

THE CREATION NARRATIVE reveals the first-ever definition of our relationship with God: He is our Creator, and we are His creatures. It shows us who God is—the majestic Creator who, out of

His tremendous love, spoke heaven and earth and all living things into being. We see God as the one who creates orders and rules, who provides and sustains. But the passage also reveals our relationship to God as His creatures. It shows us that we are loved, dependent, and equipped with free will to respond to Him through obeying His commands. Also, because we are made in the image of God, we are relational beings who are meant to be in relationships with others. In fact, we are designed to be in an intimate, harmonious relationship with our Maker so that His presence is something we can enjoy. What the Creation narrative reveals is God's original design of our relationship with Him, and with it comes several essential reminders because this Creator-creature relation is an aspect of our relationship we often overlook. Below are several implications derived from the Creation narrative that should shape our daily walk with God.

Creator and creature are distinctively different in nature

The fact that He is the Creator and we are His creatures means that God and mankind are distinctively different in nature. It is a difference that can never be overcome. Regardless of how much we are like Him, we will never *be* Him, even though we are the only creature created in His image. Some power, ability, and knowledge are meant to belong only to the Creator, and never the creature. As the Creator, He is the one who defines the world and lays down rules and boundaries; He alone has the authority and power to create, give life, judge, and destroy. God alone deserves glory and honor; He alone is to be worshipped. Nor is God bound by time or space; He is eternal and infinite.

On the other hand, we as creatures are completely dependent on God, relying on His provision and sustenance. We are flesh, made from the dust of the earth, but given life because God loves us. In fact, as creatures, we are made to follow and worship God, instead of being our own master. This is true even though we have been given dominion over other living creatures and are appointed to take care of the earth God created. Ps. 103:15–16 (NASB)

2. GOD'S ORIGINAL DESIGN

reminds us of our creaturely nature, "As for man, his days are like grass; like a flower of the field, so he flourishes. When the wind has passed over it, it is no more, and its place no longer knows about it." The stark contrast between our everlasting God and fleshly mankind is further illustrated in Isa. 40:6–8, "All people are like grass, and all their faithfulness is like the flowers of the field. The grass withers and the flowers fall, because the breath of the Lord blows on them. Surely the people are grass. The grass withers and the flowers fall, but the word of our God endures forever."

We are flesh, with our full set of limitations. We need to eat and sleep, we can be hurt, and we can get sick. Our time on earth is transient, and we have limited control of our circumstances. Indeed, many of our limitations are not because of the Fall (which will be discussed in more detail in the next chapter); it is simply because we are creatures. This is not to undermine what humans can achieve, or to deny the power of willpower that has allowed people to repeatedly overcome seemingly insurmountable limitations. After all, we are made in the image of God—with the ability to analyze and understand, and are given free will and the ability to respond. But we need to acknowledge that regardless of how hard we try, we will never be completely independent, nor will we have complete control over our circumstances. Our body has its share of limitations because we are made this way, and we need to accept this about ourselves.

We will never fully know or comprehend God, His word, and His plan

This is an extension of the previous point. Because of the chasm between God and us in terms of our nature and ability, creatures can never fully comprehend God and His plan. We will only know what God reveals of Himself, in the way He chooses to reveal Himself. But how much He decides to reveal is entirely His will and authority. Since God has chosen to reveal Himself through God incarnate Jesus Christ and His word, it means that we cannot understand God and His plan apart from these avenues. Many scholars and theologians have generated invaluable knowledge and insight from God's word, and we are all benefactors of their hard work. Yet the chasm between God and us is seen in the fact that despite human's best efforts, we still do not have adequate vocabulary and models to fully illustrate God and the many mysteries revealed in His word. One such topic is the trinitarian nature of God. While theologians have made significant progress through the centuries to come up with models to illustrate this concept, we still struggle to concretely express and enunciate the full picture.

Indeed, there will always be truths we cannot completely understand or reconcile, especially regarding topics that the Bible has only alluded to. This means that many statements or commands in the Bible will likely appear contradictory, because our finite minds will have a hard time grasping the full riches of God and His revelations. An example of a seeming theological paradox is when we try to reconcile the love and justice of God. In our minds, we cannot comprehend how one can be just *and* loving at the same time. Therefore we tend to reduce and simplify the concept by treating love and justice as extremes on two sides of a spectrum. Our inadequate understanding of God's character, in turn, affects our perception of God, causing us to have an overly simplistic view of God as primarily loving *or* just, instead of both. This difficulty is illustrated in Figure 1.

Our struggle to understand the interrelation of love and justice is also manifested in the way we attempt to live out God's command. Mic. 6:8 says, "And what does the Lord require of you? To act justly and to love mercy and to walk humbly with your God." Because we cannot seem to reconcile love and justice, we often end up choosing one side while ignoring the other. We sometimes emphasize justice to the extent of losing mercy, or we overlook justice when we focus on love. When we don't understand how God can be both loving and just, we also struggle to be both when we try to follow His command.

2. GOD'S ORIGINAL DESIGN

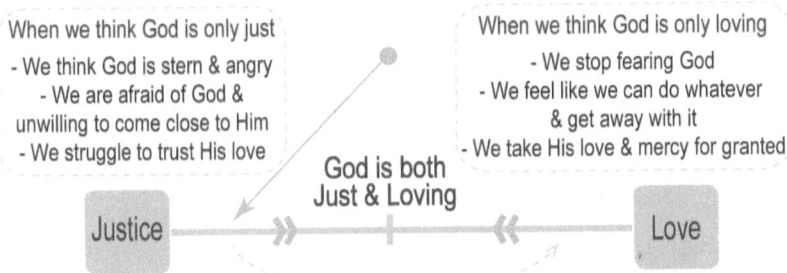

Figure 1. Because we have a hard time reconciling the love and justice of God, we tend to focus only on either the love or justice of God based on our personal preferences, while also swinging between the extremes based on circumstances.

This realization reminds us that we cannot acquire a more balanced and comprehensive view of God and many of these concepts without prayerful inquiry of the Holy Spirit. We need to recognize that despite all the knowledge we have garnered regarding God through the years, no one can claim to have God and His revelation all figured out, and we still can never interpret and understand God's revelations *apart from Himself*. We need to develop an acute awareness of the temptation to think that we humans can take these revelations as our own knowledge and be independent of God.

On the other hand, it is comforting to know that we are not supposed to understand these seemingly difficult and disjointed concepts on our own. Our finite minds will struggle with it, but we can always *pray and ask God*. Our God is a loving God who has chosen to reveal Himself so we can have a relationship with Him. He will answer us when we seek to understand His revelation, and He will know how to reveal it in a way that makes sense to us. God is still speaking today, and He will grant us new insights and meaning from the never-ending riches of His word when we continue to pray and seek.

IN A RELATIONSHIP WITH GOD

Our Creator loves and cares for us deeply

Acknowledging the utter imbalance in power and ability inherent in our relationship with God is a cause of worry for some, because it leaves us feeling helpless, like we are trapped in an unjust fate with no escape. This fear and awful feeling of inescapability is something that we will address later. But our uneasiness is rooted in the belief that our well-being is only safeguarded by *our* ability to think and act independently, and to fend for ourselves when necessary. But this is when we need to remember that God loves and cares for us deeply. Yes, He is mighty and powerful, yet in all His power, He chooses to love us—creatures created from the dust of the earth. Our Lord God is the one who created the universe and all living creatures, but He is also the one who watched over and took care of Adam and Eve so tenderly and lovingly.

The way God loves us is indeed one big mystery because He does not need to. Our God is trinitarian in nature, in that while there is only one God, God is also three persons in one (the Trinity), which are the Father, the Son, and the Holy Spirit. The three persons subsist eternally in one being, meaning the Father, the Son, and the Holy Spirit are in a loving eternal fellowship and communion with one another. Therefore, God really did not need to create us to keep Him accompanied. But He chose to create us, take care of us, and fellowship with us because He loves us.

Ps. 8:3–8 captures this mystery beautifully:

> *When I consider your heavens,*
>   *the work of your fingers,*
> *the moon and the stars,*
>   *which you have set in place,*
> *what is mankind that you are mindful of them,*
>   *human beings that you care for them?*
> *You have made them a little lower than the angels*
>   *and crowned them with glory and honor.*
> *You made them rulers over the works of your hands;*
>   *you put everything under their feet:*

2. GOD'S ORIGINAL DESIGN

all flocks and herds,
*   and the animals of the wild,*
the birds in the sky,
*   and the fish in the sea,*
all that swim the paths of the seas.

Our Lord God is not someone we need to fight. He has been on our side from day one. In God's original design, we never need to fend for ourselves because God has already taken up that role. He is our provider and sustainer, and He knows us better than ourselves because He is our Maker. He has seen and known us before we were even born. "My frame was not hidden from you when I was made in the secret place, when I was woven together in the depths of the earth. Your eyes saw my unformed body; all the days ordained for me were written in your book before one of them came to be" (Ps. 139:15–16). God uses His knowledge and power to care for us, knowing exactly what we need, because He made us. We can lean on Him, we can trust Him, we can depend on Him. Here we are reminded again that this is how we should relate to our Creator.

In God's original design, we have rules to follow and work to do

Another important realization from the Creation narrative is that the Garden of Eden is a little different from what we might have imagined. In our minds, if the Garden of Eden is the perfect place God created for us, we probably will think of a place with unlimited food, where we will not have to work, and where there are no rules to follow. Yet in God's original, perfect design, God had laid down clear commandments that Adam and Eve would need to obey using their free will. There was also work for them to do, even before the Fall. This tells us that God, being our Maker and knowing what is the most suitable for our being, has prescribed for His beloved mankind a life that is seemingly contrary to our liking. We will see why there is this discrepancy in the next chapter. But before then, we need to notice two things.

First, we as creatures are made to follow God's command

because God knows we do not have the ability to unequivocally determine what is good and evil. This knowledge belongs only to God, who alone knows what is best for us. Therefore God established rules and guidelines for mankind in the Garden of Eden because He knows that we need them to make sense of our life. After all, following the Creator's commands is our rightful response as creatures—it is how we worship Him.

Admittedly, we are not too fond of the idea that we are created to follow God's command. We feel that our freedom is compromised when there are rules to follow. Yet because we are created to follow God, we are all inadvertently following some other guidelines when we are not following Him. For many of us, our decisions are based on a worldview established by our cultures in this fallen world. We have learned the rules that our upbringing and our society have engrained in our systems, and we have knowingly or unknowingly been abiding by these rules, allowing them to dictate the choices we make. Therefore as much as we struggle to accept this aspect of our creaturely nature, we must remember that it is written into our relationship with God from the beginning. We can ask God to help us see how following His commands is inherently good and necessary.

Second, clear duties and work were given to Adam and Eve in the Garden of Eden. As discussed, they were to work the field, take care of it, and rule over creation. While we might all dream of the days when we finally stop working and just enjoy life, the Creation narrative tells us that work is not inherently bad. We all have a duty, a role to fulfill in God's perfect design. It is a responsibility, but it is also meant to bring purpose and fulfillment. We need to seek wisdom from God to delineate God's original design of work, which is beautiful and purposeful, from the many factors that may have made work a tedious burden in our lives.

In God's original design, human beings are relational in nature

Today we live in a world that values individuality and independence. Everyone wants to be true to oneself, to be seen and heard as

2. GOD'S ORIGINAL DESIGN

an individual. Relationships are often compromised to make way for personal successes and self-actualization. Furthermore, since relationships can bring so much frustration and disappointment, often we are unsure of how we should navigate our relationships. We want to be loved and accepted, but we are terrified of rejection and alienation. We are lonely, yet at times, our attempts to fit in only leave us feeling empty and exhausted. Consequently, sometimes we opt to stay away and just keep to ourselves.

But it is interesting to note that in the world God created, mankind was placed in a web of relationships from the beginning. In God's original design, we have never existed alone, nor do we exist in a vacuum. From the moment we came into being, God placed us in relation to Himself, the newly created world, and other living creatures. This is seen in God's commands to mankind: we are to be fruitful and multiply; to subdue the earth, work the ground and take care of it; and to rule over other living creatures. God's commands tell us that mankind is not just living in the world God created, but we are supposed to have relationships with the world and other living creatures, managing and working to take care of them. It shows us that relationships are not optional, but central to our being since day one. We are made in the image of God so that we can have a relationship with God and people. In fact, God made it plain that it was not good for Adam to be alone. Adam needed a companion, a fellow human being to be in a relationship with, so that together they could fulfill God's command to proliferate.

Indeed, as the creature created in God's image, the centrality of relationship is written into our being. Our God is a relational God; therefore, we are also relational beings. We are made to be in relationships because the Father, the Son, and the Holy Spirit are in an eternal relationship with each other. In fact, the relational nature of our being defines our humanity. We are human because we are capable of having relationships, and we need these relationships to make us human. This is an important reminder from the Creation narrative, to know that humans can never do away with relationships, regardless of how difficult relationships are and how much pain they cause. We need to remember that in God's perfect, original design, we are meant to be embedded in this web of relationships. It is intended to be good, beautiful, and harmonious. We must try to understand this point before we enter the next chapter that turns everything upside down.

Points for Reflection

1. When we recognize God as our Creator, we acknowledge that all humans are inevitably in a relationship with Him as His creatures, even if the relationship is broken or bad. How does this realization affect the way you view your relationship with God?
2. As creatures made by God, we are limited, dependent, and made to follow His commands per God's original, perfect design. How does this change the way you view yourself?
3. Being made in the image of God, we are relational by nature. Is this surprising? How does this knowledge impact your perception of yourself and your relationship with God?

3. BROKEN BY SIN

THE DISINTEGRATION OF OUR RELATIONSHIP WITH GOD IN THE FALL NARRATIVE

Reflection Questions

1. What do you think is the impact of sin?
2. How do you think sin affects your perception of God, yourself, and your relationship with Him?

Unfortunately, the beautiful picture at the end of Genesis 2 would soon be changed drastically. Of all the commands God gave Adam and Eve, only one was a prohibition—they were not to eat of the tree of the knowledge of good and evil. As creatures made to follow and obey God, this would be the opportunity to respond with true obedience. After all, we only demonstrate true obedience when there is a choice between obedience and disobedience, and we choose to obey with our free will. But the one prohibition would become the opportunity the crafty serpent seized to cause a rift between God and mankind. He chose to target the woman, first introducing doubt regarding God's command. "You will not *certainly* die," the snake said. Pretending to know why God would prohibit mankind from eating the fruit, he added, "For God knows that when you eat from it your eyes will be opened, and you will be like God, knowing good and evil" (Gen. 3:4–5).

The temptation presented by the serpent was the possibility of being *like God*. Mankind would be able to cross the impossible chasm that separates the Creator from the creature. And the defining feature of being God-like? Mankind would now know good and evil. This is ironic because we are already like God, being the only creature created in His likeness. But it wasn't enough to be like God; for the real temptation was to disobey God and *become God* by gaining a knowledge that is meant not for mankind, but reserved only for God the Creator.

Yet the damage was done, as we witness the serpent's lies seemingly taking on a life of its own in Eve's head. "So when the woman saw that the tree was good for food, and that it was a delight to the eyes, and that the tree was to be desired to make one wise, she took of its fruit and ate, and she also gave some to her husband who was with her, and he ate" (Gen. 3:6 ESV). Interestingly, what she saw of the tree is exactly how God described the trees that He caused to grow in the Garden of Eden in Gen. 2:9—trees that are pleasing to the eyes and good for food (even though the order of the descriptions are reversed in 3:6). But Eve saw something else in the tree; she saw that the tree was desirable because it would make one wise. This no doubt echoes the serpent's temptation, the temptation to venture beyond the boundaries set by the Creator, so that she could be wise like God. So she ate the fruit and gave some to Adam also. God's command to refrain from eating from this tree was all but forgotten.

But what happened after they consumed the forbidden fruit? It turns out the serpent was not telling a complete lie. As described by the serpent, "the eyes of both of them were opened" (Gen. 3:5; 3:7) upon taking the fruit. But the first thing they noticed, or *knew*, was

3. BROKEN BY SIN

their nakedness, which had previously caused them no shame at all in Gen. 2:25. Did they indeed gain the knowledge of good and evil? A definitive answer is not given in the Bible, even though God admitted in Gen. 3:22 that "the man has now become like one of us, knowing good and evil." But one thing Adam and Eve had definitely gained was *shame*. Shame about themselves and their nakedness, and shame that prevented them from coming before God in His presence. In fact, the two things that immediately happened once their eyes were opened were both about dealing with this newfound shame. They first made coverings for themselves with fig leaves to hide their nakedness; then, they hid away from the presence of the Lord when they heard the sound of the Lord walking in the garden.

At this point of the passage, we have the first dialogue between God and mankind in the Bible, with God asking Adam, "Where are you?" To which Adam responded, "I heard you in the garden, and I was afraid because I was naked; so I hid" (Gen. 3:9–10). Adam's response revealed that on top of shame, fear had also entered the hearts of the first humans. Notice they were not afraid because they had disobeyed God's command, they were afraid because they were naked, and they decided to hide from the Creator who made them and prepared everything for them. It was only when God asked point-blank if they had eaten the forbidden fruit that they admitted to it, and in full display in their "confession" was their reluctance to bear responsibility for their actions. Adam explained his action this way, "The woman you put here with me—she gave me some fruit from the tree, and I ate it" (Gen. 3:12). So based on Adam's response, apparently, His Maker who also made the woman was to blame for the sin committed. Sadly, the woman's excuse was no better. She said, "The serpent deceived me, and I ate" (Gen. 3:13). So for her, it was the serpent's fault.

But they knew that there would be consequences for their disobedience, as God had clearly stated in Gen. 2:17. There are consequences when God's perfect plan for His creation is disrupted by our disobedience. He cursed the serpent and announced that not only would the serpent crawl on his belly and eat dust, but God would put enmity between the serpent and woman. Hostility entered the life of mankind, and so did pain, for God would make the pain of childbirth very severe. The husband would rule over his wife. As for Adam, the ground was cursed because of his disobedience, so mankind would only eat food from it through painful toil. The ground would produce thorns and thistles (Gen. 3:14–19).

What was once natural and easy when mankind obediently followed God's command, such as the command to multiply and work the field, became difficult and painful. Mankind's relationship with the earth, other creatures, and each other was forever altered. But above all, God's relationship with mankind was broken, and humans were banished from God's presence in the Garden of Eden. God had to send an angel and a flaming sword to guard the entrance of the Garden of Eden, so that Adam and Eve would not be able to live forever in this fallen state by eating from the tree of life. It is true that Adam and Eve did not just drop dead on eating the fruit, even though God promised that death would be the consequence of disobedience. But death had, in a way, come upon them with the breaking of their relationship with God and their banishment from the tree of life, because God alone gives life. Such is the dire consequence of sin.

It is a chilling passage. It is the complete ruin of a beautiful picture, the disintegration of relationships. What God considered as "very good" (Gen. 1:31) is no more. With Adam's and Eve's choice to disobey God, the once intimate and beautiful relationship between God and mankind is broken, along with mankind's relationship with other creatures and each other. Even our relationship with ourselves is broken, as we are riddled with shame and lost the ability to accept and face ourselves with honest approval. Genesis 3 is a chilling passage because it reveals that the many things that cripple our lives today—shame, hostility, pain, conflicts, rifts in relationships, and this sense of alienation, all entered the reality of our existence during this one regrettable episode.

Yet what we must also notice from this passage is that while our disobedience broke our relationship with God, God did not stop loving us. When shame took over the lives of Adam and Eve because nakedness suddenly became a thing to be ashamed of, it was *the LORD God* who personally took care of His disobedient creatures and clothed them with garments of skin (Gen. 3:21; recall how the term "the LORD God" highlights the intimate, personal relationship between God and mankind). Even when God banished Adam and Eve from the Garden of Eden to prevent them from eating from the tree of life, it was out of love, because God could not let this fallen state become eternity. His love and care shine through despite our disappointing actions. Indeed, this love is what prompted God the Father to send His son to die on the cross for us, so that the consequence of this episode can be rectified.

IN THE FALL NARRATIVE, we see God's original design of our relationship with Him ruined by mankind's disobedience and sin. Our relationship with God is not simply one of Creator-creatures anymore, but one of Creator-*fallen* creatures. It is sadly a reality that we are still dealing with in this fallen world. As such, we must ask, how has our perception of God, ourselves, and our relationship with Him changed after the Fall? What happens when creatures seemingly gain a sense of good and evil, something that is meant to belong only to the Creator? The Bible only gives us glimpses, but several observations can be made from the passage.

The crux of the primal sin is the desire to become God

The first realization from the Fall narrative is that at the crux of the original sin is a desire to *become* God. As mentioned, we are already like God because we are made in His image. Yet we are certainly not God, and many attributes that belong only to God are not inherent to us even though we bear God's likeness. One of those attributes is the knowledge of good and evil, considering that God prohibited mankind from eating from the tree of the knowledge of good and evil. Adam and Eve knew this attribute was off-limit for creatures, but this was precisely where the temptation lay.

Therefore when mankind chose to ignore God's command and did the forbidden, the desire that Adam and Eve gave into was the desire to cross the boundary set out by God for His creature, thereby possessing something that belongs only to the Creator. It was the desire to *become* God and be our own master instead of taking our rightful place as creatures. The sin is, above all, a willful violation of God's original design, when we are no longer content with being creatures made to worship God, creatures made to be dependent, and creatures made of mere flesh.

In our fallen state, we refuse to acknowledge that only the Creator possesses the authority and ability to judge and determine what is good and evil. Therefore, from the primal sin comes the temptation of *pride*, an unwillingness to accept our role as creatures and to stay in the relationship with God as originally designed. This pride makes us think that we can be like the Creator, in the sense that we are independent and capable of deciding for ourselves everything regarding ourselves. It is this desire, and the accompanying refusal to honor God as God, that broke mankind's relationship with God. We must be aware of this temptation that still lures us away from God today.

Taking the forbidden fruit compromised our ability to see good and evil according to God's standard

If taking the forbidden fruit resulted in the opening of our eyes, if humans had indeed gained the knowledge of good and evil, then it appears that the outcome of this disobedience is that there are now two different standards of good and evil. What God saw as good, i.e., created humans who are naked, were considered not so good by the post-Fall mankind, thereby prompting Adam and Eve to rectify the situation by making coverings for themselves. In God's original design, there is only one standard of good and evil, and that standard is determined by God and God alone. After all, only God has the authority and knowledge to make accurate judgments. On the other hand, as creatures, we are supposed to rely on God's command to tell us what is good and evil.

3. BROKEN BY SIN

Yet when Adam and Eve disobeyed God and gained the false idea that humans now harbor the same knowledge as God, we think that we can tell good from evil on our own, apart from God. This is a manifestation of the pride that underlies the primal sin, a willful departure from how God intends for us to be. But we did not know that our sense of good and evil is tainted, because our conscience, granted to us when God created us in His image, is no longer informed by God's standard of good and evil. So we are left thinking we know what is best for us, instead of God.

This has serious consequences. We do not necessarily agree with God anymore concerning what is good and evil. We no longer see how God's plan of having us follow His command is good. We look at God's original design and resent that we are created as dependent and limited beings, because we want to follow our own will, according to what we think is good. We also have a hard time understanding how having this intimate relationship with God is beautiful and essential, so we cherish His blessings more than our relationship with Him. This altered sense of good and evil leaves us self-centered, as good and evil are now defined by our limited perspective.

What we are left with, in actuality, is a greatly diminished ability to follow God's commands, because we no longer think that God's way is the best. We question God's judgment and actions when we do not understand His plan, and we have a hard time trusting Him when His way is different from ours. Our alienation from God makes us think that we need to count on our ability to definitively determine good and evil, yet God's plan has always been for us to rely on Him and trust Him, because He loves us still after the Fall. Therefore we must remind ourselves of His love when we do not understand His ways. "'For my thoughts are not your thoughts, neither are your ways my ways,' declares the Lord. 'As the heavens are higher than the earth, so are my ways higher than your ways and my thoughts than your thoughts'" (Isa. 55:8–9). None of us are supposed to comprehend God's plan fully, but if we are ever in doubt, the reminder here is to trust His love.

The Fall resulted in shame that cripples mankind's ability to engage in truthful, intimate relationships

The most notable change after the Fall was for Adam and Eve to suddenly be cloaked in a tremendous sense of shame. It was a shame that left them scrambling for coverings for their nakedness, a shame that pushed them to hide from their Creator. This is significant on two levels. First, the need to conceal themselves revealed a newfound difficulty in accepting themselves for who they were. They could no longer accept that their creaturely bodies were naked, and they were ashamed of it. It is almost as if the way God created them was not good enough anymore, and this prompted them to hide who they were by concealing themselves.

Unfortunately, this is a sad situation that still rings true today. So many of us walk around with this sense of shame, or to express it with terminologies we are more familiar with, a deep sense of inadequacy and insecurity. We feel like we are not good enough, not smart enough, not successful enough, not lovely enough. Many argue that this is the result of how we are conditioned in today's competitive society, in a world that thrives on comparison. But this yearning of wanting to be accepted and told that we are good enough does not go away even with endless achievements and recognition. It is a horrible feeling deep inside us that stems from being alienated from the loving God who loves and accepts us.

Second, this sense of shame further damages mankind's relationships, because we are now afraid of presenting ourselves just as we are. Shame caused Adam and Eve to hide from the presence of the Lord, withdrawing from their relationship with God even before they were banished from the Garden of Eden. They could not face up to themselves or God, and the distance they put between themselves and God through actual hiding or lies only caused a further rift in their relationship with God. Indeed, when we are no longer comfortable with open honesty in a relationship, it cripples our ability to be in an honest, intimate relationship, regardless of whether it is with God or other people. When true intimacy is missing in our relationship with God and others, it only leaves us

3. BROKEN BY SIN

feeling lonely and unaccepted, further causing us to be guarded and shallow in our relationships.

For many of us, this sense of inadequacy and alienation still dictates how we relate to God today. We see God as someone we need to counter and guard against, instead of someone on our side. The fact that God knows everything about us as our Maker is a cause for fear rather than comfort because we naturally want to keep parts of ourselves hidden. As fallen creatures, we lost the ability to trust that we can still be worthy and loved, just as we are. We cannot believe that God loves us just the same when He knows all about our creaturely nature and our sins after sin enters our world, because sometimes we have a hard time loving and accepting ourselves as well.

But Jesus did not die on the cross for mankind before the Fall. Instead, it is precisely because of the Fall that we need salvation. With Jesus's death and resurrection, God declares that all of us, with our flaws and sins, are worthy because He calls us worthy. Jesus came so our relationship with God can be restored to how it was before the Fall. Jesus's sacrifice reminds us that regardless of who we are and how we have been, we are loved and worthy. There is no need to hide or put up a facade or let insecurities take control of our lives anymore. In our restored relationship with God, He will slowly bring healing and growth if we open our hearts and trust Him.

Pain entered our world, turning God's original design into sources of suffering

The final consequence of the Fall is the entry of pain and suffering into mankind's existence. Pain is now attached to the tasks God assigned to mankind. Childbirth and working the field will be painful; food will come only with painful toil all the days of man's life. Mankind will no longer be able to enjoy God's provision like they used to. Not that God has stopped providing and sustaining —God still provides the rain and the soil, and the field will still produce food; it is just not unlimited and effortless anymore. Accompanying the breaking of mankind's relationship with God is the disintegration of mankind's relationship with others in God's creation. The ground is cursed and will no longer be productive like it used to be; there is now enmity between the serpent and woman. Marriage will also have new challenges because the husband will rule over the wife. We suffer and are hurt when our relationships are in disrepair because relationships are such a central part of our being.

Every beautiful thing God has intended for mankind turned sour. God created work so that we can have a sense of purpose and fulfillment as we take up our duty in His plan, but it has become a source of stress because it is no longer easy. Compound that with our insecurities and a desire to feel worthy through our achievements, and suddenly work becomes a burden that is too heavy to bear. On the other hand, marriage is meant to be where humans experience the fulfillment of an intimate relationship and companionship. But in our fallenness, marriage will be marred by power struggles and inherent inequality. Our difficulty in engaging in honest, intimate relationships also further strains our marriages. Yet regardless of how grim the situation seems, we must remember God's original design and His beautiful intentions, and not condemn work or marriage altogether. God can help restore our relationship with work and others when we remain in Him. This is the comfort we can have as God's children.

Points for Reflection

1. When we realize that at the core of the primal sin is pride and a refusal to live according to our place in God's design, how does this impact the way you view sin, both sin as a concept and sin in your own life?
2. When we think of our sins, we are usually afraid of the punishments God may bring. Yet in Genesis 3, we see that the first consequences of sin, before God's rightful

pronouncement of their punishments, were shame and fear, an inability to accept oneself, and the need to hide. Do you see how this sense of inadequacy and the tendency to withdraw still plague your life?

3. Even when Adam and Eve failed to obey God, God did not stop caring for them. The relationship was broken, but God still loved them. He loves us the same way today. Have you experienced God's love and mercy, even in your sins? Pray and ask God to show you, and write it down in your journal so you will not forget.

_____

4. REVELATION THROUGH JESUS
LEARNING TO RELATE TO GOD THROUGH JESUS'S EXAMPLE

Reflection Questions

1. We know that God is love, and He loves us tremendously. But if you are to describe how God has loved you, what will your answer be?
2. Now that our relationship with God has been restored with Jesus's sacrifice, how is this restored relationship manifested in your life? What are some examples that represent this restored relationship in your spiritual journey?

The Fall narrative is a gloomy episode. In three chapters of Genesis, we went from a God-centered existence to a self-centered one, and so much of the pain and helplessness we know today came from this

4. REVELATION THROUGH JESUS

regrettable incident. The good news is that God knows how to fix this. Jesus has already died on the cross for our sins, so that we can be on the path of healing and redemption from the horrific consequences of the Fall. Our trinitarian God is not just our Creator anymore, but also our Savior and Lord. On the other hand, we gain the new identity of redeemed sinners when we choose to place our faith in Jesus Christ. Our relationship with God has been restored, and we can again come before Him and fellowship with Him the way Adam and Eve did in the Garden of Eden. We can begin to live a God-centered life, reclaiming our role as God's beloved creature made in His image. In His grace and mercy, we will slowly accept ourselves as we are—fallen, merely flesh, yet deeply loved.

However, simply because we have been reconciled to God does not mean that we automatically know how to *be* in this restored relationship. Yet we need to look no further, for Jesus has demonstrated with His life how we are to relate to our heavenly Father. In this chapter, we will focus on insights we can obtain from Jesus's teaching and His relationship with God the Father to help us navigate our relationship with God.

Jesus's relationship with the Father precedes the Son's role as our Savior in history

When we look at the life of Jesus, we are often drawn to the many actions and works of Jesus's ministry on earth. We see Him performing miracles, raising the dead, casting out demons, and teaching with authority and insights that could only have come from heaven. We see Him dying on the cross in utter obedience and being raised from the dead on the third day to bring God's plan of salvation to fruition. But it is important to note that Jesus's actions were all deeply rooted in His relationship with God the Father. Their relationship was there *first*, before there were actions and missions, because He has been in an eternal fellowship of love with the Father and the Holy Spirit. Jesus said this of His Father, "You loved me before the creation of the world" (John 17:24). In addition,

Jesus said in John 10:30, "I and the Father are One." What Jesus said in these verses gives us a glimpse of the eternal fellowship enjoyed by the Holy Trinity. Indeed, as previously mentioned, relationship is central to the being of our trinitarian God, for the three distinct persons are eternally in a relationship with each other as the Father, the Son, and the Holy Spirit, never separate or independent from each other.

This intimate relationship between Jesus and the Father is further illustrated by a distinctive phrase Jesus used. He said, "I am *in* the Father and the Father is *in* Me" (John 14:11). It describes a kind of relationship that is far beyond our understanding of a close relationship. It is not simply a sense of intimacy that comes from feeling understood, supported, and loved. Instead, it describes a state of mutual indwelling, an intimacy characterized by an openness to honest sharing and a willingness to let the other person into our lives. This level of intimacy enables a unity in knowledge, will, and action among the Holy Trinity as one God.[1] The Son, the Father, and the Holy Spirit are one, and this relational foundation precedes all the work Jesus did during His time on earth.

Jesus's intimate relationship with the Father is characterized by tremendous love and knowledge

When we take a closer look at Jesus's relationship with the Father, the first thing we notice is that their relationship is characterized by tremendous love. The Father said this of Jesus during His baptism, "This is my beloved Son; with whom I am well pleased" (Matt. 3:17 ESV). It speaks of the Father's love and approval for His Son, and it is a declaration of Jesus's unique identity—that He would be the costly sacrifice that makes salvation available to all. In fact, the Father's love for Jesus is repeatedly mentioned in the Gospel of John (John 3:35; 5:20; 10:17; 15:9; 17:26). It is worth noting that two Greek verbs of "love" are used to describe the Father's love for Jesus: (i) phileo, which denotes love and devotion based on emotions and is closer to our usual understanding of the word "love"; and (ii) agapao, which denotes love and devotion based on will.[2] This means

4. REVELATION THROUGH JESUS

that the Father does not just love Jesus with affection, as in He genuinely likes and loves to be with His Son, but He also loves Jesus with His choices and actions, using His will. More importantly, we see that the love between the Father and the Son is mutual. Jesus expressed His love for the Father by saying, "But I do as the Father has commanded me, so that the world may know that *I love (agapao) the Father*" (John 14:31 ESV). Therefore, this relationship is, first and foremost, a relationship of mutual love.

Second, we notice that their relationship is characterized by immense knowledge. On one level, we see Jesus knowing detailed "facts" about Himself and the Father, such as His own identity and that of the Father's, and the kind of relationship they share. We see Jesus harboring explicit knowledge about His mission on earth, and the Father's role in His mission. Jesus declared His Father as the one with the sovereign authority to judge, to give life, and to raise from the dead. The Father is also the one who initiated the plan of salvation, and the one who sent Jesus to bring it to fruition (John 5:17). On the other hand, Jesus was fully aware that He is the Son sent by the Father to do the Father's will, to reveal God and speak His words, and all authority has been given to Him by the Father (John 5:22, 27; 6:38; 17:1–2). He acknowledged that everyone who would be saved was given to Him by the Father, because even though Jesus Himself is fully God, He could never do it apart from the Father (John 1:18; 6:37, 44, 46; 8:28; 12:49–50; 14:7).

But the knowledge we see in many of Jesus's descriptions is beyond head knowledge. It speaks of the kind of knowledge that is gained during interaction and fellowship in an actual relationship. It speaks of Jesus knowing full well how much the Father loves Him, why His Father loves Him, and what He could do to express His love for His Father. This is the kind of knowledge that comes only with genuine interaction and time spent together in a relationship. Jesus used the verb "know" to describe the intimate knowledge you gather about the other person when you interact with honesty and openness in a committed relationship. Jesus said in John 10:15, "The Father *knows* me and I *know* the Father." The Greek verb "know" not only refers to intelligent comprehension, as in coming to understand, but it also refers to getting to know a person, and gaining a level of certainty through experience.[3] The super-intimate relationship experienced by the persons within the Holy Trinity enabled Jesus to harbor such immense and accurate knowledge about the Father, Himself, and their relationship. It also allowed Jesus to know about the Father's will and their respective roles in Jesus's mission.

Jesus's intimate relationship with the Father is expressed as a unity in will and action

For many of us, love and knowledge are passive in nature. Love is often pictured as a feeling in our hearts that we may or may not act upon. The same is true with knowledge. We are all bombarded by a wealth of knowledge daily, many of which never impact our decisions or actions. Nonetheless, the love and knowledge in Jesus's relationship with the Father are anything but passive. Rather, the mutual love and knowledge between the two result in a unity in *will and action*. When Jesus knew about the Father's will, He reacted by doing God's will in obedience. There are multiple instances in the scripture where Jesus's stated knowledge of the Father's will is followed immediately by Jesus declaring that He would act in obedience, as if knowledge and obedience are one and inseparable. Jesus said in John 8:55, "I do know Him (i.e., the Father) and obey his word." Similarly, after Jesus mentioned how He and His Father know each other in John 10:15, it is followed by the phrase, "and I lay down my life for the sheep," referring to how Jesus would later die on the cross in obedience to the Father's will.

These examples show that Jesus did not allow His knowledge about the Father's will to remain as head knowledge, but responded with actions. Of course, we can attribute Jesus's utter obedience to His sinless nature, but Jesus Himself gave a reason for this obedience. He said in John 14:31, "I *love* the Father and do exactly what my Father has commanded me." Jesus followed the command of the Father because He loves the Father. Obedience was thus Jesus's way

4. REVELATION THROUGH JESUS

of expressing His love for the Father; it is a love expressed through actions, actions that would bring glory to the Father (John 17:4).

But Jesus is not the only one expressing His love through actions. The Father's love for Jesus is seen in how He prepared Jesus for His mission. Indeed, the love of the Father is the reason cited for the many preparations He made when Jesus was sent. For example, the authority with which Jesus performed miracles and brought salvation was given to Jesus *because* the Father loves Him (John 3:35). This love is also what prompted the Father to show Jesus all that He was doing, so Jesus could follow suit (John 5:20). In His love, God the Father made sure that when He sent Jesus on this journey, Jesus would be well equipped.

This mutual expression of love through actions results in a positive cycle, where Jesus's obedience feeds into the Father's love and deepens this fellowship of love. This positive cycle is described in John 10:15–17, where after Jesus declared that He would lay down His life, He said, *"The reason my Father loves me* is that I lay down my life." John 15:10 paints a similar picture, with Jesus stating that obedience is how He is enwrapped in God's love. "I have kept my Father's commands and remain in His love." Jesus's relationship with the Father is, therefore, one that is rooted in tremendous love and immense knowledge that comes from intimate sharing and fellowship. This results in a unity in will and action because they chose to act on this love by taking up their respective roles in the relationship—the Father being the one who prepared His Son, and the Son acting in obedience. It is a beautiful picture demonstrating the love between the Father and the Son when they act in harmony and unity.

BUT WHAT CAN we learn from Jesus's relationship with the Father? Are we supposed to relate to God the way Jesus relates to His Father? The answer would be yes, because Jesus has repeatedly illustrated that His relationship with the Father is analogous to our relationship with Him and the Father. First, the same preposition, "in," is used to describe our relationship with Jesus and the Father. Jesus said to His disciples, "On that day you will realize that I am *in* my Father, and you are *in* me, and I am *in* you" (John 14:20). Furthermore, Jesus stated that the Holy Spirit is also *in* us (John 14:17). It describes the intimate relationship we are supposed to have with each person of the Holy Trinity, in a way that is comparable to the relationship the Son has with the Father.

In addition, the way Jesus and the Father harbor mutual knowledge of each other is analogous to the knowledge we should share with Jesus. When Jesus referred to Himself as the good shepherd, He said, "I know my sheep and my sheep know me—just as the Father knows me and I know the Father" (John 10:14–5). We share with Jesus a deep knowledge of each other, the way Jesus and the Father know each other in their relationship. It reveals that through being "in Christ," we as believers are given the privilege to participate in the intimate relationship and fellowship among the Holy Trinity. Somehow, in God's love and will, we as creatures get to participate in this intimate fellowship of love. Jesus's relationship with the Father will give us the pointers we need to learn to relate to God, and this is what we will discuss next.

We are all deeply loved

The first reminder we can garner from Jesus's relationship with the Father is that our relationship with God, too, is rooted in tremendous love. Each of us is deeply loved. The Father loves us the way He loves Jesus (John 17:23), not just with His will, but He likes us and loves us affectionately. Jesus also loves us with the same love, because He said, "As the Father has loved me, so have I loved you. Abide in My love" (John 15:9 ESV).

Unfortunately, most of us are not fully aware of how much we are loved. The fact that our God loves us so much is something that takes a moment to sink in, because we are so used to the world telling us that we are not good enough. It is unimaginable that even though we sometimes have a hard time accepting ourselves for who we are, God loves us, fully accepts us, and is very fond of us. In

4. REVELATION THROUGH JESUS

addition, whatever He calls us to do, He will equip us to ensure we can complete the task He sent us to do. In our relationship with God, we can experience the love and acceptance we crave, and the tender care and faithful protection by our heavenly Father, who never stops watching over us. This is a love only God can give, a love that comes upon us only because Jesus's sacrifice restored our relationship with the triune God. This is the most precious gift.

We will grow in our knowledge of God, ourselves, and His will

Second, as we stay in Christ and our relationship with God deepens, we will also grow in our knowledge of who God is, who we are, and what it means to have a relationship with God. Jesus said in His prayer to the Father, "I have made you known to them, and will *continue* to make you known in order that the love you have for me may be in them and that I myself may be in them" (John 17:26). It speaks of an ever-increasing knowledge that is associated with our intimate relationship with Jesus. We will come to know God as the almighty being who is loving but also just, the God who is faithful and merciful but also sovereign and holy. We will see how much the Father loves the Son, and how much the Father loves us. It shows us our true identity as creatures to our Creator, as redeemed sinners to our Savior. We will learn to discern the will of God, to know what pleases Him. It is a process whereby head knowledge learned from reading God's word becomes knowledge written on our hearts, and we grow to truly *know* God and ourselves more and more.

We are to respond to God's love with our actions

Third, as our knowledge of how much God loves us grows, we will learn to respond in love through our actions. We see from the example of Jesus and the Father that love is not separate from actions. We might sing songs about how much we love God (not to discount genuine moments of worship), but Jesus's life makes it clear that if we indeed love God, we respond with actions. It is very plainly stated in John 14:15, "If you love me (i.e., Jesus), keep my commands." It is an important realization, especially for many of us who view keeping God's commandments simply as an obligation. On one hand, we *are* supposed to keep God's commands, because it is the rightful response to our Creator and Lord. But Jesus's example shows us that, above all, this is how we express our love to God. We follow His commands because we know that this pleases Him.

At this point, some might wonder whether it is still important to keep God's commands if we are already loved and forgiven just as we are. This is because we are so used to the idea that if we are loved and accepted, there is no need to change or do anything. But in actuality, this question exposes our misconception about love, and sadly only reveals how we might have taken His love for granted. God loves us, that is certain, but do we know how to love Him? If our focus is only on what we will gain from the relationship without seeing how important it is to respond to His love with our obedience, how can we say we love God? Our obedience is not how we secure His love; it is how we express our love. Isn't this the gist of an intimate relationship, where we care not only about ourselves but also others, and we do what makes the other person happy not because we have to, but because we want to? We are called into this fellowship to respond in love; let us respond through our actions by keeping God's words.

In addition, John 14:21 says, "Whoever has my commands and keeps them is the one who loves me. The one who loves me will be loved by my Father, and I too will love them and *show myself to them*." A similar message is repeated in John 14:23 (NASB), "If anyone loves me, he will follow My word; and My Father will love him, and *We will come to him and make Our dwelling with him*." These verses describe an increase in knowledge, intimacy, and love in our relationship with God when we respond to God's love by keeping His word. When we keep His word, God will abide in us. The word "abide" describes an intimacy that is a state of being, a state where the Father, the Son, the Holy Spirit, and we are all stably dwelling in this intimate fellowship (John 14:17, 20). Thus, it depicts a positive cycle where the more we keep His commands, the more we are stably dwelling in this intimate fellowship of love with our

4. REVELATION THROUGH JESUS

trinitarian God. John gives us an apt summary in 1 John 2:5–6 (ESV), "but whoever keeps His word, in him truly the love of God is perfected. By this we may know that we are in Him: whoever says he abides in Him ought to walk in the same way in which He walked."

More importantly, as much as we are called to respond to God's love with our actions, we are never meant to do them on our own. We see from Jesus's example that in everything He did, He learned from the Father and did them with the authority given to Him by the Father. God would never leave us on our own to live a life that is pleasing to Him. Jesus said, "As the branch cannot bear fruit by itself, unless it abides in the vine, neither can you, unless you abide in Me" (John 15:4 ESV). Thus, the more we choose to respond to God's love by keeping His commands, the more we will know God, and our intimacy with God will continue to grow. As we remain in Him, we will learn more about drawing on God's strength to bear fruit and respond with our actions. In God's perfect design, our intimate relationship with Him precedes our actions, where the relationship per se will grant us everything we need to live in a way that further deepens this relationship of love. It is a never-ending growth and deepening of our love and relationship with God, as we dwell in the love and presence of God. There is nothing more beautiful and precious than this.

Points for Reflection

1. Very few people are completely happy with themselves. We always wish to be better, whether it is our physical features, personalities, or abilities. Yet God loves us and accepts us just as we are. How does this realization affect the way you view yourself? Do you realize how precious and cherished you are to our heavenly Father?

2. If our relationship with God is characterized by the love and knowledge that come when we spend time with Him, how will you change the way you approach your faith so that you will truly know Him and His love?
3. If loving Jesus is responding with our actions, think of one aspect of your life where you can put this into practice by choosing to honor His will instead of your own. Write that down in your journal, and ask God to help you follow through on this prayer of dedication.

_____

5. APPLICATION: WALKING WITH GOD
KNOWING GOD, OURSELVES, AND THE KIND OF RELATIONSHIP WE SHOULD HAVE WITH HIM

Reflection Questions

1. What kind of images comes to mind when you try to picture your relationship with God? Are you a child with a loving father? Are you a servant with your lord? Or are you a sheep with the shepherd? Try to describe the picture you have in mind.
2. What is the biggest challenge you face when trying to walk with God?

So how can we put all the information from the previous chapters back into our daily walk as Christians? How are we to build upon our identity as fallen creatures saved by grace, or assimilate what we learned from Jesus's relationship with the Father into our journey of faith? As mentioned earlier, to know how we should relate to God and walk with Him, we need to have a consolidated understanding of who God is and who we are. Yet this is no small feat, as revealed by our discussion up to this point, because our relationship with God is built on multiple identities and relations—as Creator and creatures, as righteous God and sinners, as Savior and redeemed sinners. Not only have we unknowingly been emphasizing some identities over others, but we are unaware of how important it is to consolidate these different perceptions of God and ourselves into an integrated, coherent picture. Consequently, our understanding of God and ourselves is incomplete, which leads to confusion when we come across bible passages that appear to portray God and ourselves in a different light. Therefore this chapter aims to put together a consolidated understanding of God and ourselves, followed by several practical reminders to help us grow deeper and steadier in our relationship with God.

Who is God in our relationship?

We have been introduced to different images in the Bible to help us relate to God. A few examples would be the images of God as our shepherd, heavenly Father, Creator, our Lord, etc., some of which are images we have discussed in previous chapters. However, as mentioned, these images have remained as disjointed notions in our heads. There are several reasons behind this. First, while different images are used to emphasize different aspects of God's character, we often have a hard time reconciling seemingly inconsistent attributes of God. How could God be loving and merciful like a shepherd or a father, but also readily brings judgment and punishment like a lord or master? We do not know if we should look at God as someone warm and personal, whom we can run to for an embrace, or someone cold and distant, with whom we need to be on our best behavior at all times so we are not punished. As a result, most of us subconsciously emphasize certain attributes of God over others, choosing to see God as either loving *or* stern, and settle with a discounted understanding of God.

5. APPLICATION: WALKING WITH GOD

Second, our interpretation of these images is often influenced by many things in addition to how they are used in the Bible, such as our culture and personal experiences. Take the term "heavenly Father" as an example. While for some, it may elicit an image of a loving father who protects and cares affectionately; for others, it brings to mind a stern, authoritative figure who rebukes and disciplines. Another example is the term "lord," which recalls the image of masters who exploit and deal harshly with their servants because these are the images we have from our cultures (current or historical). But our interpretations are not necessarily consistent with the portrayals in the biblical text, thus making it even more difficult for us to see how these images can be reconciled.

Third, we often allow our understanding of the Holy Trinity to be completely segregated. We think that God the Father is the stern one because He is the one who created the world and brings judgment. Jesus, on the other hand, is the loving one because He died on the cross for us. Then we forget that the Holy Spirit who dwells in us is also fully God, whom we need to revere and love. But even with the many images presented in the Bible, regardless of whether it is associated with God the Father, the Son, or the Holy Spirit, there is only one God. The Holy Trinity may have different tasks, but they have the same attributes because they are *one* trinitarian God. Therefore in constructing a coherent picture of who God is, we need to unpack some commonly misunderstood images of God to clarify and consolidate our understanding of God.

Creator

An easily misconstrued image of God is that of Him as our Creator. We usually think of the Creator as a powerful God who is infinite and cosmic, but too cold and distant to care about our well-being, or we might think of Him as a powerful God who exercises complete authority over us, who readily punishes us when we fail to act in obedience without considering our struggles and limitations. As discussed in Ch.2, our God is indeed the powerful, majestic, and infinite God who created the world by speaking everything into being. He is the one who established the rules of the world as we know it—the trajectory of the sun and stars, the changes of the seasons, and the working of the ecosystems. He created creatures large and small, including us, and established the boundaries and relationships among His creation.

Yet this does not mean that our God is too great and powerful to care. Instead, the Creation narrative shows us that our God cares deeply about us and His creation. In God's perfect design, humans lead an existence of complete dependence on God in a fellowship of love. As our Creator, He knows us, provides for us, sustains us, takes care of us, and gives us work to grant us a purpose.

But our God is also Holy and just. He alone decides what is good and evil; only God fully knows and understands how destructive sins are to His beautiful creation. In His holiness, God has no tolerance for sins; any deviation from His standard will bring consequences and judgment. Therefore God gives us commands to follow, because first of all, it is inherent in our role as creatures to obey and follow our Creator and worship Him. But the commands are also God's way of protecting us because God knows that sins bring consequences.

Indeed, we see the heart of God when Adam and Eve disobeyed God and sinned in Genesis 3. Although they received their fair share of punishment because of their disobedience (a consequence for which they had been forewarned), God did not stop caring for them in His love and faithfulness. He made garments of animal skin to clothe them and guarded them from the tree of life so they would not live forever in the fallen state. Here we see a God who is holy, mighty, majestic, to be revered, but also loving, good, and faithful, who chooses to love us deeply and made us so we can fellowship with Him. This is the unchanging character and will of God.

Shepherd

For many believers, the image of the shepherd captures the love of God. This is because most of us think of a shepherd as someone who kindly and gently leads his sheep to green pastures, protecting

5. APPLICATION: WALKING WITH GOD

them from harm and danger. While this is undoubtedly part of what a shepherd does, there is much more to his role. Integral to the shepherd's role of guiding his sheep is the need to discipline them and correct their path. He needs to make sure that they listen to his voice and walk accordingly, even if it means using the rod and the staff. So even with such a loving image, the element of justice—as in all disobedience of the stray and wandering sheep will be corrected—is also there. In fact, similar to what the term "Creator" implies, the image of the shepherd also speaks of a relationship of total dependence. The sheep rely on and trust the shepherd completely. Thus while "Creator" and "shepherd" appear to portray two vastly different gods at first glance, similar attributes are actually present in these images.

Father

The same is true with the image of the Father. This is a tricky one because it is typically so heavily influenced by our relationship with our earthly fathers. But a general expectation of a father would be someone who provides for us and takes care of us, as in raising us and giving us food and shelter (although sadly, this may not be the case for many). But beyond that, our perceived way of interacting with our father can be quite different. Some think of a father as someone who is warm and affectionate, who cares so much about our happiness that he is ready to answer to all our needs, almost to the extent of spoiling us. Others picture a father who is stern and authoritative but more distant, who is all about discipline and ensuring that we are on the right path to excel and achieve in life.

But our heavenly Father is different. He is authoritative and will certainly discipline us when we disobey His commands, yet at the same time, God also loves us warmly and affectionately. Recall that in Ch.4, we talked about how the Greek verb "phileo" is used to describe the way the Father loves Jesus. It refers to the kind of love that is warm and affectionate, where you enjoy being with this person because you are so fond of them. This is how God loves us too. He looks at us fondly and lovingly, the way we want to cuddle and cherish a cute baby or a lovely puppy. It might be difficult to imagine that God would love us this way, but that is what the Bible has portrayed for us.

The image of the Father shows us a God who provides for us, sustains us, protects us, and wants what is best for us. But He also knows how to love us without spoiling us and how to discipline us when necessary, because He is loving and wise. It is the juxtaposition of God's love and justice, an element also found in the image of the Creator and shepherd.

Lord

Another example is the word "Lord," which is used frequently in the Bible. In the Old Testament, it is used in place of the four-letter name of God (YHWH) and is usually written in all upper case letters. In the New Testament, it is most frequently used to refer to Jesus. As believers, we have all confessed Jesus as Lord. But because the word "Lord" also means masters, for many of us, it recalls the image of masters. Indeed, this term helps us understand the lordship of Jesus in our lives as the ruler and master of our lives. It reminds us that we belong to Jesus, and He should be the object of our devotion, the one we follow and serve. It highlights the reverence we should have for our Lord, who has the power and authority to give us directions and tasks to finish, but could also punish us when we fail to respond in obedience. This is consistent with our understanding of God so far because it emphasizes God as someone we need to respect and obey.

Unfortunately, this term sometimes also brings the inaccurate perception that we will be dealt with harshly by our Lord, with every mistake punished unjustly, because we have seen too many examples of masters exploiting their servants and treating them unfairly. But the Bible has made it clear that masters are to treat their servants justly and fairly, and with the fear of God (Col. 4:1; Eph. 6:9). A good lord protects his servants and provides them with food and shelter, and will manage his servants with love and justice. Not to mention the Lord we have is Jesus Christ—the Lord who

5. APPLICATION: WALKING WITH GOD

knows us, understands us, and loves us so much that He died on the cross for us. In fact, Jesus said we are more than servants (John 15:15). Therefore, the image portrayed by the word "Lord," when understood correctly, still describes God as someone who loves us, takes care of us, and treats us justly, although the emphasis is more on us recognizing that we belong to God and should follow and serve Him alone.

A coherent picture

In summary, we see that while each of the terms used to describe God specifically highlights an aspect of God's role in our relationship, they all reveal a similar picture because there is only one God. God, in His divinity, is indescribably greater, more powerful, and far superior than we are. Our God is sovereign and majestic and to be revered. But God is also loving, merciful and good, choosing to love us and take care of us (and discipline us when necessary) in a fellowship of love. Furthermore, as discussed briefly, we need to realize that different persons in the Holy Trinity harbor the same character because they are one God. We see that the picture portrayed by the term Father, which obviously is associated with God the Father, is consistent with that illustrated by the image of the shepherd, which has been associated with God in Ps. 23, but also with Jesus in John 10:11–15. The Holy Spirit, on the other hand, is our Helper who teaches us and comforts us, but also rebukes us and convicts us of our sins to keep us on track (John 16:7–8, 13–14). All three persons of the Holy Trinity are portrayed to love us, guide us, take care of us, but also discipline us.

In addition, while each person has a slightly different role, they act in unity to help us and watch over us as one God. An example is the image of the vine. We are the branches connected to Jesus the vine, which the Father prunes to make us more fruitful, while the Holy Spirit who dwells in us keeps us connected by reminding us of the teaching of Jesus (John 14:26; 15:1–2). This is how our trinitarian God loves us and takes care of us. May our understanding of Him be defined not by culture or our earthly experiences, but be transformed by His words and our own walks with Him.

Who are we in our relationship with God?

If God has defined our relationship as one where God and we are not equals, but He is the one who guides us, watches over us, provides for us, and disciplines us, then what does this say about who we are and how we are supposed to relate to God? Not many of us have asked this question, and it sounds a little too philosophical when we first hear about it. But deep down, we all have an image of ourselves that will heavily impact the way we interact with God. Think of a child who feels loved and cherished, versus one who feels like they are still not good enough, and you can imagine how these two kids will interact very differently with their respective parents. The same goes for us believers. When the Bible tells us that God loves us, are we behaving as children who are beloved, or are we still desperately trying to win our heavenly Father's approval? On the other hand, if we are loved and forgiven, does it mean we can do whatever we want in our lives, because Jesus's blood has already paid for all our sins?

We are creatures dependent on a loving God

If God's design is for Him to be the Creator who loves us and takes care of us, then the first thing we must acknowledge is that we are creatures made to be completely dependent on a loving God. As creatures created in God's image, we have been given the ability to reason, respond and act according to our free will. Nonetheless, we are also made to depend on God, to fellowship with Him and follow Him, instead of leading a life apart from Him.

This is a fact that might be difficult for us to accept because of two reasons. First, we are raised to believe that our identity and value come from our independence and achievements. Indeed, the very temptation Eve succumbed to during the Fall was the desire to become God. It is the temptation to break free from God, make our

5. APPLICATION: WALKING WITH GOD

own rules, and determine our values because we believe we know what is best for us. In our fallenness, we detest the idea that we have to be dependent, let alone dependent on a God who is beyond our control.

But thinking that we can be independent of God is a lie, first told by the serpent. The Bible reminds us that, as creatures, we are limited and frail. Our existence is transient, and our effort to leave a mark is often futile. "The life of mortals is like grass, they flourish like a flower of the field; the wind blows over it and it is gone, and its place remembers it no more" (Ps. 103:15–16). James 4:13–14 states it very plainly, "Now listen, you who say, 'Today or tomorrow we will go to this or that city, spend a year there, carry on business and make money.' Why, you do not even know what will happen tomorrow. What is your life? You are a mist that appears for a little while and then vanishes." Whether we acknowledge it or not, God has been the one sustaining us and protecting us. He is the one who gives us life. He has sustained the world we are in, a world where food can grow, where there are water sources and a change of seasons. He has sustained and protected us in one way or another in each of our personal lives, many of which we took for granted. We must stop believing this lie and realize that God, in His love, has been taking care of us this whole time.

Second, we do not like the idea that we are dependent creatures because, deep down, we find ourselves unworthy just the way we are. As discussed in Ch.3, the first thing the Fall brought was a sense of shame. We secretly despise our creaturely nature—frail, limited, unable to control our circumstances—and we wish we were more. We thought we would finally be worthy if we could be smarter, better-looking, richer, more popular, or more accomplished. Making the matter worse is that as sinners, we continue to sin daily despite being saved, and we are left to wonder, how could anyone love a dependent creature who is merely flesh and cannot stop sinning? Even by our human standards, we may have a hard time finding ourselves lovable, let alone a God who is incomparably greater than us. But God loves us, as unimaginable as it may be. He chooses to love us just as we are, wanting to fellowship with us, even when we are His enemies. In fact, He sustains us and cares for us precisely because He knows we are merely creatures. He really *is* love. His love permeates through all the sins and doubts.

In fact, it is only in His love that we will be able to slowly break the spell of sins and believe in this ground-breaking truth: we are worthy because God, who made the rules of this universe, calls us worthy and precious. We are valuable because we are God's beloved creation made in His image—not only that—but our worth is demonstrated unequivocally by Jesus's choice to salvage us through His costly death. Contrary to what our cultures are telling us, our value has never been about the mark we leave on earth; rather, it lies in the value God bestowed upon us in His love.

When the Bible speaks of the fleshly and transient nature of our existence, the aim is not to shame us and tell us that we are worthless. In Ps. 103:15-16, the discussion of man being like grass is immediately juxtaposed with the everlasting love of God in the next verse (Ps. 103:17), "but from everlasting to everlasting the Lord's love is on those who fear him."[1] Yes, our existence may be transient, but our God loves us with everlasting love. Therefore we must stop trying to rely on ourselves to make ourselves worthy. Instead, look to God, and be in awe of His love! This sentiment is beautifully captured in Ps. 144:3-4, when the psalmist exclaims, "Lord, what are human beings that you care for them, mere mortals that you think of them? They are like a breath; their days are like a fleeting shadow." How wonderful it is to know that God's opinion of us, unlike the world's, never changes.

We are sinners who have been given the strength to change

But accepting our identity as dependent creatures loved by God is only the first step in knowing who we are in our relationship with God. In God's plan of salvation, we are also given strength and courage to face our sins and overcome them, because God sees how much suffering sins bring and He loves us too much to let us stay as helpless sinners. Thus, while God knows all about our struggles, flaws, and sins, and fully accepts us in our fallen state, He does not

5. APPLICATION: WALKING WITH GOD

want to leave us there. God knows that it is only in our restored relationship with Him that we will have the guidance and strength we need to overcome sins' grip on our lives. Jesus has risen from the dead, and our victory has been won. We can change because with Him, we can. Nothing is too difficult for our almighty God.

Therefore the second part of knowing our identity in our relationship with God is acknowledging that while we are sinners, and will remain so until Jesus's return, we have been freed from the bondage of sin and given the strength to live differently during our time on earth. We no longer need to wallow in self-pity and self-doubt, because God has chosen to love us even though He knows every good and bad thing we are capable of. We can rest in God's love knowing that our value is secure, because it is defined by God and not the world or our behavior. Yet, at the same time, being assured by His love gives us the courage and strength to rise above this feeling of helplessness. It gives us hope that we can overcome the bondage of sin and be victorious. By relying on God's strength instead of ours, we will finally be able to respond to God's love with our actions, choosing to live in a way that pleases God.

Still, we must remember that learning to break free from our sinful nature is a lifelong journey. It is a constant battle because we will inevitably succumb to our old, sinful ways of life and grieve the Holy Spirit. In times like these, the Holy Spirit will remind us, and God may discipline us. Our first instinct may be to run from God and hide from Him, just like how Adam and Eve responded. But this is when we must remember God's love for us again and anchor our identity in His love. Our heavenly Father is someone we can trust and rely on because He understands us and knows how to help us. In fact, it is only with God's strength, not ours, that we will be able to choose to follow the Spirit and not our flesh.

When we come before our Creator and Lord and acknowledge that we need His help, when we come with a willing heart wanting to repent from our sinful ways and ask for forgiveness, He will help us (I John 1:9). We will not only experience His acceptance and love anew, but we will be given new strength to live differently. Our attempts to live godly lives will no longer be our ways to earn God's love, but a reaction, a response to His love. When we do that, what we will see and experience is a relationship of receiving and reciprocating, even though we are only giving what we have received from our gracious God.

A coherent picture

So who are we in this restored relationship with God? It is acknowledging two seemingly paradoxical aspects of our identity. On the one hand, we are to acknowledge that we really do not have anything to boast about. We are creatures made from dust who are never meant to lead an existence apart from God, even though we are made in God's image. We are merely flesh, limited, and completely dependent. We have fallen short of the glory of God, and there is nothing we can do to earn our salvation.

Yet, on the other hand, God has decidedly chosen to love us despite everything we are. In fact, He has never stopped loving us, from when we were made, to when we fall, and even when we continue to grieve Him every day. In His love, our God who is just and holy chose to grant us salvation through the sacrifice of Jesus, so that we are justified and placed on a path of sanctification. In our restored relationship with God, we can go back to recognizing ourselves as creatures made to worship our Creator, sheep to be guided and protected by our shepherd, and children to be loved and taken care of by our heavenly Father. It is ceasing to be our own master, but allowing God to be our Lord by humbly acknowledging His authority to discipline us, determined to live a life pleasing to God as an expression of our love.

It is a mindset that is at the midpoint of two extremes. It is recognizing that we are secure in God's love, knowing that we are valuable and cherished because our worth is based on God's faithful love. Yet, at the same time, we do not take His love for granted and stop fearing God, foolishly choosing to go back to our old way of life, thereby letting sins regain control of our lives and grieve the Holy Spirit. Hopefully, with time and God's grace, we will realize that our identity can only be understood in relation to God, and it is only in our relationship with God that we experience the love, intimacy, understanding, and acceptance we long for, because we are made to fellowship with God this whole time.

Reminders for our walk with Him

WHEN WE UNDERSTAND God as the one who made us, knows us, saves us, loves us, protects us, and disciplines us; when we acknowledge that we are redeemed sinners and beloved creatures made to fellowship with God, then we can see that our relationship with God must be one of *total dependence and trust*. A rightful relationship with God means relinquishing our desire to be our own master, and instead choosing to honor God by trusting Him, following Him, and worshiping Him in a fellowship of love. When we continue to abide in God, we will grow in our knowledge of God and ourselves. We will learn to trust God's good and perfect will and act in obedience. Furthermore, our hearts will be increasingly filled with the peace, joy, and hope that comes with trusting and obeying God in this intimate and loving relationship. This is the blessing God has in store for His children, regardless of how our relationship with God has been. Below are several reminders to help us live out our restored relationship with God, so that we can experience the abundance God has promised.

Allow the relationship aspect of our faith to inform our lifestyle as Christians

The first realignment we need to make is recognizing that our restored relationship with God is not just an additional item to tackle amongst the slew of activities we do as Christians. Instead, it is at the center of our Christian faith because it is the context, the framework through which we make sense of the commands and teachings from the Bible. When we let this "relationship mindset" inform how we comprehend and live out our faith daily, it brings new meaning and coherence to the practices and perspectives we inhabit as followers of Christ.

Take reading the Bible as an example. We might have looked at it as something we are supposed to do diligently as Christians. But when we understand the Bible as God's way of revealing Himself, and hence how we can get to know God, we will see that it is not something we do to be good Christians, but how we cultivate our relationship with God. Indeed, when we take a step back and think about what a relationship entails, we will recognize that in any relationship, the relationship grows when the two parties get to know each other—through spending time together, talking, and sharing. The same is true for our relationship with God. When we read and study the word of God, when we listen to sermons and go to Sunday school, we are, in fact, cultivating our relationship with God because we are getting to know Him.

Similarly, the act of praying is given new meaning when we understand it as our way of dialoguing with God. When we pray, not only are we coming before God and quieting down in His presence, but prayer is how we share and open up our lives to God. It is a crucial way for us to interact and communicate with God, and thus also how our relationship with God deepens. When we reconsider prayer from a relationship perspective, it reminds us that praying is so much more than us asking God for help and provision in times of need. It is acknowledging that God is our personal Lord with whom we can share our thoughts, problems, and joys. It is inviting God into every aspect of our lives by honoring and seeking His opinion and input on our daily happenings, because we trust that He hears our prayers and will respond with wisdom, love, mercy, and righteousness. When prayer is understood this way, it frees us from getting too fixated on whether our prayers are "heard" or "answered" because the act of praying is an end in itself. Indeed, God hears all our prayers; He simply may not answer them the way we want. After all, our heavenly Father knows all our needs, with the Holy Spirit interceding for us even before we know to pray for ourselves. We can trust in the love and goodness of God.

Like any earthly relationship, a relationship is hardly good or

5. APPLICATION: WALKING WITH GOD

growing if the two parties never even talk. So if reading God's word is hearing what God has to say, and our prayers are responding and continuing with the dialogue, then both are critical for our relationship with God. It is through these exchanges that we learn to interact with Him as redeemed creatures worshipping and fellowshipping with our Creator, Savior, and Lord. It is also only in personal time spent with Him that our relationship grows and deepens. May we experience the intimacy and joy God intends for us as we learn to share with Him and enjoy His presence.

It is a change that takes commitment and discipline

But if all we need for our relationship with God is reading God's word and praying to God, why is it important that we join a church? This is because the difficulty associated with living out this restored relationship is something that cannot be underestimated. Learning to walk with God is, after all, a large shift in values, mindset, lifestyle, and action. We are used to running our own lives and relying on our resources to solve our problems, but now we learn to honor God as our Lord, coming to God to seek His help and trust Him in every aspect of our lives. It is a change that involves not just taking on a new approach to life, but first letting go of the old, familiar approach. Therefore if it takes discipline to start even a diet, imagine the commitment and discipline it takes to participate and grow in our relationship with God.

This is why believers are encouraged to join a church or a cell group because unless we consistently allow ourselves to hear and talk about God, very soon, God and our relationship with Him will be all but forgotten. The world we are in is so loud. It constantly bombards us with values and information that are contrary to how God wants us to live. We are drawn to and tossed around by the temptations of the world. Only when we have a group of believers and a schedule that helps us stay close to God that we will be able to maintain our focus on God and our relationship with Him. We all need help to remain aware of His presence every minute of our lives, so that our relationship with God, one that has eternal value, will not be left on the sidelines.

Our Relationship with God is a lifelong journey, not an endpoint

With all the discussion emphasizing the importance of having a good relationship with God, it is very easy to view it as a goal to be achieved or an item to be checked off. We might even consider a good relationship with God a badge of our spirituality and proof that we are doing well as believers. But there is something inherently detrimental with this understanding of our relationship with God, because treating it as something we want to excel at distorts the very nature of it and prevents us from experiencing its true beauty. A relationship is, by definition, a journey (and in our relationship with God, a lifelong journey), not an endpoint that we accomplish and move on from. The substance of a relationship is found precisely in the continuous, everyday interactions we have with God—in the moments that are shared, and the understanding and trust that are nurtured. A relationship is meant to be experienced, not assessed and labeled as good or bad. When we are constantly gauging how good the relationship is, it takes our focus away from the interaction itself and turns our relationship with Him into a personal achievement.

In addition, trying to objectively gauge whether a relationship is "good" is more difficult than we think. We each have slightly different ways of interacting with God based on our personality and upbringing, and our definition of what makes the relationship great may differ. Not to mention our personal perception of whether the relationship is going well often fluctuates. Haven't we all experienced periods in our lives when we feel incredibly close to God and empowered by His love, and yet there are also phases when we feel uninspired and distant? Sometimes this is indeed caused by us drifting from God and not spending time with Him, but there are also times when we have prayed and read His word diligently, yet God feels silent and far. These instances remind us that we must not define our relationship with God *only* by our experience or a feeling

5. APPLICATION: WALKING WITH GOD

of intimacy. Rather, it is about *an intention to remain committed to* the relationship, because what Jesus asks of us is to *abide* in Him. This is part of what it means to be faithful in our lifelong relationship with God—to continue coming before God, to continue to pray, to continue to read His words, to not walk away and give up—even though at times, we have our doubts and God feels distant.

When we focus on remaining in Christ and experiencing our relationship with God, our relationship will grow, like the fruit we bear as believers who abide in Him. It helps us remember that an intimate relationship with God is a result of God's grace, not something we achieve on our own. In fact, recognizing God's grace in this relationship steers us from the temptation of pride that comes from thinking that we have excelled in it through our own effort. This unhealthy mindset gives us the wrong impression that we are spiritually superior to other believers, which tempts us to stop relying on God while also judging others, even though there is no way for us to fully assess their relationship with God. May God guard our hearts so that we see more of His grace and less of our effort and input in our relationship with Him.

Open up, be patient, and trust Him

Another aspect of our relationship with God being a lifelong journey is that our understanding of God, ourselves, and our relationship change and evolve with time. This is true on two levels. First, we will gain more knowledge and information about God, His character, or who we are when we continue to read His word and delve deeper into the riches of His revelation. Second, as much as our perspectives are renewed with new information, there is a difference between knowing it in our heads and experiencing it in our hearts. It will take much longer to internalize such knowledge and assimilate it into our being, to truly *know* God and how we are to fellowship with Him.

Take the love of God as an example. It is one thing to read about the love of God or to hear about it from others' testimonies, but it is something else to experience His tender care and provision in our own lives. This is why it is essential to remain in Christ because it takes time for us to experience the reality of this relationship in our lives. It is a process that requires us to learn to open up to God, to stop hiding from Him so that He can transform us from within, because this change comes not from us absorbing more information, but from interacting and fellowshipping with the living God.

When we understand that this growth is a lifelong process, an important reminder that will help us navigate this journey is to be patient, whether it is being patient with the process, or being patient with ourselves. Admittedly, patience is not our strong suit in a world that prides on efficiency and instant gratification, but it is paramount in our relationship with God. As fallen sinners, we still carry with us the shame that entered our lives during the Fall episode, which hinders our ability to fellowship with God in a truthful, intimate manner. We are insecure and uncomfortable with who we are and naturally want to hide instead of opening up.

Therefore learning to share with God and open up to Him is not only a conscious choice we need to make, but there will be a learning curve that we need to be patient with. It is no easy feat because it goes against our instinct. There will also be times when we are tempted to compare with others who seem to have progressed further and faster. Yet we cannot afford to let sin, shame, or frustration get in the way of us coming before God, because in Him alone is the healing touch that will slowly release us from our insecurities. God loves us just the way we are, and He is inviting us to come before Him with open arms. He who knows us inside and out also knows how to help us grow at our own pace, in our own way. We can trust God and His timing.

As we open up to God and form the habit of sharing with Him our feelings, worries, or things we may not have told anyone, as we continue this journey and do not give up, slowly but surely, our lives will be transformed. We will come to accept and love ourselves the way He does because we have experienced His acceptance and kindness. We will get better at recognizing God's voice and seeing His hands in our lives. We will be much more attuned to the

5. APPLICATION: WALKING WITH GOD

guidance of the Holy Spirit, learning to love what God loves, and once again appreciating His standard of good and evil. We will learn to trust God's love and goodness more, even when the situation seems abysmal and there appears to be no way out of our problems. Every difficulty will be an exercise to give our burdens and worries to Him, trusting that He is taking care of them. Every trial is an opportunity to trust God instead of ourselves, to trust that His solutions are higher and better so that we respond with obedience. With time we will learn to relish the ease that comes with depending on God and striving with His strength instead of ours. It is a never-ending cycle, but with every round, we grow closer to Him and to who we are supposed to be in God's original design.

Again, this does not mean we will finally graduate from our relationship with God and be completely independent. That is our earthly notion of growth. Instead, we will grow to be more and more dependent on God and His love, learning to lean on God as our faith grows. Maybe with time, we will finally learn to cherish and celebrate our dependence on our heavenly Father, recognizing that this is what intimacy looks like and where our joy, peace, and hope are supposed to come from.

Relationship before works

So far, we have talked surprisingly little about works and actions, the things we do as believers. Not that these are unimportant. We saw from Jesus's example that His intimate relationship with the Father is reflected in a unity in their will and actions. Jesus has also made it clear in John 14:15, "If you love me, keep my commands," indicating that action is an essential manifestation of our relationship. Indeed, as we grow in our relationship with God, we will be better at discerning God's will, and with the help of the Holy Spirit, we will be able to live a life that is more aligned with His will.

But it has been left until now because as Jesus has demonstrated for us, our relationship with God must precede the works we do. We need to know how to *be* in our relationship with God before we know what to *do*. This does not mean that we sit around and wait for our relationship with God to mature before we start living for Him, because God intends for us to begin living a Spirit-led life once our relationship with Him is restored. But relationship precedes works because it is only through our relationship with God that we learn to act and work with God's strength instead of ours. As portrayed by the image of the vine, the branch is joined to the vine before fruit comes forth. Similarly, our actions must also be rooted first in our relationship with God and this fellowship of love. Thus, our actions and works are not only a response and reflection of this relationship, but an overflowing of the love and grace we received from God. This awareness protects us from the trap of pride and a false sense of independence, which leads us to serve with our own strength, eventually leaving us susceptible to burnout.

Before we continue, nonetheless, it is crucial to quickly discuss what constitutes "works and actions." In the minds of many, when we talk about the things we do as believers, we think of ministry-related tasks, such as joining the worship team, the usher team, and the refreshment team. Or we think of serving God as preaching the gospel, helping the poor, or entering full-time ministry. These certainly are all ways to serve God. But when Jesus said, "If you love me, keep my commands," He is referring to a much broader scope of actions. Keeping His commands is not just about actions we do to serve God, but it is in how we live our lives. Jesus gave an example in John 15:12, "My command is this: Love each other as I have loved you." So when we think that we are serving God by feeding the hungry, maybe what is even harder to do is loving our brothers and sisters, especially the ones we don't get along with. We have all struggled to follow God's commands, and more so than ministry, we too can burn out trying to live a life that is pleasing to God when these efforts are not rooted in our relationship with Him.

This is why it is so important that we learn to fellowship and communicate with God as we respond to His love with our actions. Jesus asked the Father to send us the Holy Spirit because it was never God's plan for us to do it on our own. Even Jesus never did it alone; it was always done with the strength of the Father. But one of the reasons we serve with our own strength is because we are not

5. APPLICATION: WALKING WITH GOD

adequately aware of the presence of God, nor are we used to serving with God's strength. This is a habit and an awareness that we need to cultivate—to know that God is always with us. He knows everything that happens and understands how we feel, and He is the mighty God who loves us. In Him are all the solutions and help we will ever need because He is so much bigger than any situation we are in. So let us form the habit of lifting our problems to God before seeking help from anyone or anything else, because when we seek Him with a willing heart, He knows how to help us live out our faith. After all, why would God say no to a prayer that asks for help to do His will?

Watch our hearts

As this chapter comes to a close, the final reminder is to watch our hearts. Jer. 17:9–10 says,

> *The heart is deceitful above all things*
> *and beyond cure.*
> *Who can understand it?*
> *"I the Lord search the heart*
> *and examine the mind,*
> *to reward each person according to their conduct,*
> *according to what their deeds deserve."*

Most of us begin our services in church or any efforts to serve God with good intentions. But as time goes by, when our ego is challenged, when our feelings are hurt, when we are exhausted, our motives can become muddled with selfish ambitions. It is an unfortunate outcome, an opportunity that the devil preys on to destroy the good work that God is allowing to flourish. Situations like these are unfortunately more common than we think, and it might be disappointing from a human angle, but it reminds us all the more how important it is to stay in Christ and rely on Him completely. Ask Him to search our hearts, and He will let us know if there are sins that are hidden, hurts that need healing, and disputes to be resolved. Nothing restores our relationship with God like honest repentance, when we admit to God that we have slipped and claim forgiveness through Jesus's blood. God is always faithful to restore our hearts and our strength. When we steadfastly choose to abide in Christ, the Father will prune us and help us bear more fruit. This is the promise.

Points for Reflection

1. What is the biggest surprise for you in our discussion of how we should view God, ourselves, and our relationship with Him? How will this affect the way you interact with God from now on?
2. Which of all the reminders mentioned regarding our relationship with God is the most challenging for you? We all face different struggles when we try to grow in our relationship with Him, yet regardless of what these challenges may be, God is asking us to come before Him with our struggles and seek His help. Write down the specific hurdles you are dealing with, and pray for God's guidance and strength to help you overcome them. He loves and knows you, and nothing makes Him happier than seeing you come to Him and ask for help to do His will.

SPECIAL TOPIC: THE LOVE AND JUSTICE OF GOD

"If God loves us, doesn't it mean that He fully accepts and tolerates even our flaws, so that we will never need to change?"

"How could a loving God also be associated with words like wrath and judgment?"

If the relationship between God and ourselves is rooted in love—of us knowing how much God loves us and learning to love Him with our actions, then it is critical that our perception of love is aligned with the biblical understanding of love. Nonetheless, there is often a gap between our definition and the way love is portrayed in the Bible because our understanding is inevitably shaped by our culture and upbringing. In fact, this discrepancy makes it more difficult for us to see and appreciate God's love, because it is different from what we would expect. For many of us, love is a feeling, a sense of connection, or an attraction. Beyond that, we believe that true love means unconditional acceptance. It is accepting the flaws and weaknesses of the ones you love, while granting them room and freedom to be who they want to be. Indeed, we all harbor a deep yearning to be accepted and loved unconditionally. We wish to be told that we are all right just the way we are, and that all our mistakes are forgiven. We long for this safe haven where we know we will always be cherished and loved, especially when we often feel inferior and battered in this fast-paced and competitive world.

When we compare our perception of love and what we know about God's love, we will notice that there are similarities. Indeed, the safe haven we long for has already been granted to us when Jesus died on the cross. Despite all the sins and mistakes we have made, God said we are worthy, worthy to be saved. Our sins have been forgiven and will be forgiven whenever we come before God in honest repentance, because our relationship with God has been restored when we call Jesus our Savior. However, as mentioned previously, it will take much longer for our hearts to truly understand and experience His love, because this kind of love is so rare in a broken world. Therefore we are hesitant and fearful, unsure of whether God truly loves us, because we have been hurt and disappointed. This is the first reason we sometimes experience this odd divide where we know in our head that God loves us, but at the same time, we also feel a little uncertain about it.

But another reason that contributes to this divide lies in the gap between God's love and our understanding of love. Maybe you have wondered about the following: if God loves us, doesn't it mean He fully accepts and tolerates even our flaws, so we will never need to change? Then why are we still called to repent from our old ways of life, and why would He discipline us? While we may not be aware of it, these questions actually come from our earthly definition of love. We feel that being asked to change signifies an inability to accept our flaws; thus, it is not love. Yet this is not how God loves, nor how God looks at our sins and weaknesses. God knows that a fresh start where all our previous sins are forgiven is not enough, because life on earth continues. After all, what good is a clean slate if we are repopulating it with sins and regrettable things? This is why God helps us, reminds us, and disciplines us, so that we won't have to go back to our old way of living.

SPECIAL TOPIC: THE LOVE AND JUSTICE OF GOD

In fact, what is difficult to understand about God's love is that it is a love that is also *just*. Not only do we see love and justice as opposites that are seemingly mutually exclusive, but our earthly understanding of love is often deprived of justice. We want love and unconditional acceptance to be the reason for ignoring the presence of sins in our lives. We want them overlooked and tolerated, even if we are also aware of their negative impacts, because we feel so helpless about them. However, when we only want to be loved and accepted without considering how our sins impact others, or the effort it takes for others to bear with us, this "love" is self-centered and lopsided. When love is not rooted in truth and righteousness, when we do not acknowledge that sins ultimately drain and destroy, even if tolerated because of love, we are left with merely a shadow of what love really is.

This is why God who loves us will not pretend that everything is fine or that sins are not there. He will help us change because He cannot let sins ruin our lives and the lives of those around us. His love is not seen in Him just accepting us and then not doing anything about it, and letting us wallow in our old ways of life. Instead, it is seen in His intention to help each of us, even when He knows full well of our sins and weaknesses, *because He has already accepted and welcomed us*. Contrary to common belief, God's call for us to repent and change is not a negation of His acceptance. Unlike people who try to change others out of selfish reasons (such as to suit their preferences) or when they mistake individual differences as shortcomings, God's plan to help us change is actually a manifestation of His love. Our Creator who made us knows us, accepts us, and loves us for who we are, but will also show us the sins in our lives so that we can overcome them with God's strength. We must not confuse God's love with other earthly examples.

When we understand the simultaneous importance of justice and love, we will have an easier time understanding why our loving God is also associated with words like wrath and judgment. Admittedly, when we think that love is grace and forbearance, we are taken aback by biblical accounts of God punishing disobedient people. We feel that God is too stern, too dictatorial. But we have forgotten that God, as the Creator, has every authority to decide the rules, and our role as creatures is to obey. In addition, being so used to sins we no longer see how vile, destructive, and toxic sins are. We are only terrified of the idea of judgment because we know that we ourselves have fallen short of God's standard and deserve punishment. Yet God's judgment is how today's fallen world will be given its fresh start when all evil is put away for good. Not to mention God has already provided a way out for us because He loves us.

Therefore, what these biblical accounts of God's judgment reveal is that while God loves us, His holiness is not something to be violated and taken lightly. Indeed, when we see how God could have reacted to our sins but didn't, we are only reminded all the more of His love, patience, and tolerance. We, in turn, must beware of taking God's love for granted, thereby losing sight of how we should fear Him.

OUR GOD IS LOVE, and He is also just. It is His nature. In everything He does, His love and justice shine through. With many things that happen in our lives or our world, we may not always understand how God could be both loving and just. Sometimes we cannot understand why God would allow certain things to happen. Unfortunately, often when we fail to understand, we doubt. We doubt His love and His goodness. But it is at times like these that we need to remember that as much as we think that we can tell good from evil, it was never our place as creatures to do it. We will never be able to figure out how much of it is a consequence of sins, our own or others, or how much of it is God's sovereign will. So many factors are at play in these situations, just like what we have observed time and again in our lives and in the history of the world.

Instead, maybe we should come humbly before God and tell Him our sadness, our anger, our frustration, how we are lost, and how we are not sure what to think. We hang on to the one thing we can hang on to—our relationship with our heavenly Father, who is mighty, loving, and just. When we return to God as His beloved, fallen creature, we can trust that in God's faithfulness and love, He will speak to us, comfort us, carry us through, and show us the way forward, even if we may not fully understand and see the solution ourselves.

Part II
A Community of God's Children

Up to this point, we have focused exclusively on our individual relationship with God. But this by no means suggests that our daily walk with God is only about our personal relationship with Him. In fact, it is paramount to note that there is a second, equally essential aspect, namely our role as God's Church in a fallen world. While separate sections have been devoted to these two aspects, the two are actually deeply connected and intertwined. Tackling them separately, nonetheless, allows us to gain a more thorough understanding of where we stand in our relationship with God, which is an important starting point for living out our calling as God's children. We must be rooted in God *before* we can actively take up our role as members of God's kingdom. Otherwise, we risk reducing our faith to a set of ethical rules, while also setting ourselves up for disillusionment and exhaustion when these efforts are not rooted in our relationship with Him. Therefore having discussed our individual relationship with God in the previous section, we are ready to delve into our role as God's community in anticipation of Jesus's second coming.

Most Christians are likely quite familiar with this second aspect of our faith. Many books and countless sermons have been devoted to the role of the Church in the world. We all know that as God's Church, we are to spread the gospel and bring people to Christ. Many churches and Christian organizations are at the forefront of social welfare, education, and humanitarian efforts in times of need. Increasing attention has also been devoted to preserving our environments and wildlife as believers recognize our God-given role to take care of the world. We are continuing the tradition of not looking only to our own interests but also to the interests of others, a tradition started by the early church centuries ago. We are familiar with the two greatest commandments, which instruct us to love God and love others as we love ourselves. Many take these teachings to heart and try to live a life pleasing to God. So in a way, we are familiar with this aspect of our Christian walk, maybe even more so than what was covered in the previous section.

IN A RELATIONSHIP WITH GOD

We are meant to be one community

But when we reread part of the New Testament where specific instructions are given on how we should live as members of God's kingdom, we realize that our typical understanding is missing certain elements. First, we have largely underplayed the community perspective of our Christian walk. We are all rightly concerned with how each of us ought to live, but these moral guidelines are not meant for personal achievements, so that we can excel at them and pride ourselves on being "more spiritual" than others. Instead, what we have often overlooked is how Jesus intended for all His followers to live as *one community*. We are meant to be branches attached to the same vine; there is only one Church, with Jesus as the head. The commands were given to help believers grow and mature, so as to preserve the unity and holiness of our community. We are meant to be God's witnesses as one, bringing glory to God as one.

Admittedly, this is a frustrating topic. The history of the Church, marred by centuries of disputes and divisions, is the very demonstration of how difficult Jesus's command is. We all have our share of disillusionment with our churches. So many people are hurt and taken advantage of in none other than our Christian communities. We are all so different; we are from backgrounds and cultures that clash and contradict, and we all have different personalities and priorities. We have disparate ways of interpreting things and doing things. We disagree on topics that range from doctrines to detailed steps and approaches for completing many tasks. Instead of saying that we do not know that Jesus wanted us to be one, maybe deep down, we have just given up. It takes too much effort and too many compromises, so we focus on being the best Christian we each can be—except this is only half of what God commanded.

Therefore even though it is seemingly impossible, even though it is messy, and even though it is painful, we will try to discuss in subsequent chapters how we as believers are meant to be one community. We will take into account the relational nature of our

II. A COMMUNITY OF GOD'S CHILDREN

being and how our personal relationship with God factors into our relationship with others.

We are meant to be one community in anticipation of Jesus's return

A second element often overlooked in our lives as members of God's kingdom on earth is the fact that the Church was established in anticipation of the end time when Jesus returns. The Church is to be the bride of Christ, holy and blameless, eagerly awaiting Jesus's return so that we can be united to Him in eternity. The Church will join our God in His glorious triumph when the final victory is won, and we will share in His glory as we witness the new heaven and new earth. It is a beautiful picture, but it is unfortunately not on our minds most of the time. After all, our lives on earth give us enough trouble to keep us firmly engrossed in our daily happenings. We are all fully occupied, if not overwhelmed, by the demands of our daily existence, as we try to juggle our job, family, friends, and chores. We do not even have enough time to think about our lives on earth, let alone our eternal lives that come afterward.

Moreover, it is uncomfortable for most to think about the end time. It is terrifying and filled with uncertainties. We know Jesus will come with an ultimate victory, and we will marvel at His glory. But beyond that, we are not told much more in the Bible. We wonder if the things we love on earth will still exist in heaven, and we ask about what we will be doing. We try to picture what eternal life looks like, but we are not entirely sure if it is all that exciting. We understand in our heads that judgment is coming, but we never let that thought sink into our hearts. It is a perspective that has little impact on how we approach our lives on earth because it is too heavy and too morbid. We think life is meant to be fun and to be enjoyed. But as we will see in the upcoming chapters, having an eschatological perspective is crucial. It is meant to inform every aspect of our lives and determine our priorities. We will examine the challenges we face and how we may let the eschatological mindset guide our daily walk as members of God's kingdom in the last part of the book.

6. THERE IS ONLY ONE COMMUNITY
JESUS'S COMMAND FOR HIS CHURCH

 _____

Reflection Questions

1. Do you consider yourself a committed member of a Christian community? If yes, how do you feel about your community? If no, what has kept you from joining one?
2. What do you think a Christian community should be like? What makes it distinct from other communities?

_____

In Ch.4, when we examine Jesus's relationship with the Father, the objective is to zoom in on the Father-Son relationship so that we can learn to relate to our heavenly Father. As mentioned, this allows us to selectively focus on our personal relationship with God, which is a crucial foundation and anchor for living a life pleasing to Him. But when we return to some of these passages in the Gospel of John, we will notice that as much as we are learning about our relationship with each person of the Holy Trinity, in the same breath, Jesus was also teaching us about our relationship with other believers. It is as if our relationship with the trinitarian God is essentially *one* with our relationship with fellow believers—where the two are meant to be linked and continuous, with one affecting the other and vice versa. Indeed, our relationship with God determines how we relate to others, whether it is with those within the Church or those outside the Church. In this chapter, we will focus on several passages to help us understand Jesus's command for His Church, especially regarding our relationship with our brothers and sisters.

There is only one community, and all who accepted Christ are in it

In the first part of the book, we spent a lot of time discussing the gift of salvation offered to us through the sacrifice of Jesus Christ. In John 10, Jesus used the analogy of a shepherd and His sheep to talk about how we can enter the sheepfold and become God's people. Jesus stated in John 10:9 that "I am the gate; whoever enters through me will be saved." What Jesus was referring to is that there is only one way into the kingdom of God, and that is through faith in Jesus Christ. When we enter the sheepfold, we also have a new identity because we become Jesus's sheep. Jesus is a good shepherd because He owns His sheep and loves us so much that He laid down His life for us. This analogy describes an intimate relationship we each have with Jesus, because not only does Jesus know us and we know Him, but we also know our shepherd's voice and will follow only Him.

Yet what we have often overlooked is the fact that in John 10:14, when Jesus said, "I am the good shepherd. I know my own and my own know me" (ESV), *my own* is actually used in the plural sense in the original language, Greek. So even though we usually read this verse as a description of our individual relationship with God, which is not untrue because each of us *is* Jesus's sheep whom He knows and loves, here Jesus is referring to His *many* sheep as *one*

6. THERE IS ONLY ONE COMMUNITY

entity. We all belong to Him because we have all entered the gate through Him. This is why in John 10:16, Jesus went on to talk about other sheep that are not of this fold, those who also listen to His voice, which He must bring—because there is only one flock, one shepherd. Jesus was foretelling that gentiles, despised by the Jews at the time, would one day be accepted in Jesus's sheepfold, and they would become one.

In this passage, we see a seamless extension of our personal relationship with God into our relationship with other sheep in the sheepfold. Precisely because we have all entered God's kingdom through the same and only shepherd, Jesus Christ, we are in the same sheepfold whether we acknowledge it or not. Yes, we are all very different, and we all came to know Christ differently, but we are one flock, and this is God's intention.

Yet our relationship with other believers extends beyond being fellow sheep sharing the same sheepfold. Using the analogy of the vine, Jesus reminded us that we are branches joined to the one true vine, Jesus Himself (John 15:5). Again, this analogy describes the loving and intimate relationship we each should have with our trinitarian God. But it also illustrates the fact that when we, the individual branches, are all connected to the vine, Jesus, through faith, we are all joined together into *one body* because there is only *one vine*. Paul reminds us in 1 Cor. 12:13, "For we were all baptized by one Spirit so as to form one body—whether Jews or Gentiles, slave or free—and we were all given the one Spirit to drink."

When we each remain in Jesus and Jesus remains in us, the branches are also intricately connected to each other, with the Holy Spirit dwelling in each of us. As we each participate in the fellowship of love within the Holy Trinity through our restored personal relationship with the trinitarian God, we have also inevitably entered into fellowship and communion with our fellow brothers and sisters. This is the unity Jesus prayed dearly for during His final prayer to the Father (John 17:11). This is also the unity we are reminded of with the Holy Communion, as we all partake of the same body and blood of Jesus Christ to remember His sacrifice that gives us life and brings us into this community.

These passages describe the shedding of old distinctions when we take up our new identity as Jesus's disciples and become one community because of this new identity. We are reminded that when we accept Christ as our personal Savior, we are not just embarking on a new way of life with a restored personal relationship with God, but we are saved *into a new community*, the Church of God with Jesus Christ as the head. Our conversion and being part of God's community happen simultaneously; there was never the option of accepting Christ without joining the Church of God. Concurrent with the restoration of our personal relationship with God is the induction of our relationship with other believers, whom we now call brothers and sisters. This notion often escapes our minds, but it is crucial. We need to realize that the way God looks at the Church is different from our typical perspective. He sees each of us up close, He sees how we interact with each other, but He also sees us as one Church in a bird's eye view kind of way. He has plans and expectations of us as one community. This is what we will focus on next.

A community of love, humility, and servanthood

If there is no way for us to be a believer and not be a part of God's community, then the next question we must ask is, how are we to interact with fellow believers in this community? To answer this question, we will turn to the final moments Jesus shared with His disciples—Jesus's community on earth that would later grow into the Church. Knowing that the hour of His departure was fast approaching, Jesus did something that caught everyone by surprise. He started washing His disciples' feet. "So He got up from the meal, took off His outer clothing, and wrapped a towel around His waist. After that, He poured water into a basin and began to wash His disciples' feet, drying them with the towel that was wrapped around Him" (John 13:4–5).

It was unexpected, with Peter even refusing it initially, because this task was typically reserved for women, children, and gentile slaves (even Jewish slaves were exempted from this duty). What Jesus

6. THERE IS ONLY ONE COMMUNITY

did was thus a display of humility and servanthood that was inconsistent with Jesus's social standing as their teacher and Lord. It was a display of love that would forever be imprinted in the minds of these disciples, because it was a display of love that was felt and experienced, a final act of gentleness, intimacy, and affection. It would later also be a shocking revelation of the depth of Jesus's love, when they realized that Jesus even washed the feet of Judas Iscariot, the person who would betray Jesus and bring about His death on the cross.

Jesus did the unexpected because He needed to demonstrate the true essence of His community. His community is meant to be a community that is marked by *love, humility, and a servanthood attitude*, where we count others more significant than ourselves (Phil. 2:3). Jesus went on to explain to His disciples the meaning of His action in John 13:14–15, "Now that I, your Lord and Teacher, have washed your feet, you also should wash one another's feet. I have set you an example that you should do as I have done for you." Jesus was asking them to display a love and humility that transcends social norms and worldly expectations. Jesus was saying, serve, not according to what and how much people expect you to, but exceed that. More importantly, do this not because it will bring recognition and praise, but do it out of love. Jesus's command to love is made plain in John 13:34, "A new command I give you: Love one another. As I have loved you, so you must love one another." This command is later repeated in John 15:12, with Jesus explaining what love is by stating in v.13, "Greater love has no one than this: to lay down one's life for one's friend."

The community established by Jesus is to be a community of love, humility, and servanthood, because at the core of this community is the sacrificial love of Jesus. We only get to be a part of this community because in His love, Jesus has redeemed every one of us by giving us a gift of love we don't deserve. He humbled Himself and took on the form of a servant, even though He is God (Phil. 2:6–8). Jesus has died for each of us, and He is calling us to love our brothers and sisters as people we are willing to die for, recognizing that they are precious because they have been redeemed with the blood of Jesus.

But there is more to Jesus's commands when we examine it in more detail. We need to recognize that Jesus was only asking for something He Himself has done and demonstrated. Before He asked His disciples to wash each other's feet, He was first to wash their feet. When He commanded us to love one another, it was "as I have loved you." Two observations can be made that deserve our attention here. First, when Jesus said to love one another as I have loved you, Jesus was saying that He has shown us *how* to love and *how* to serve. Jesus was asking us to emulate Him, learn from His example, and love in the way He loves. Second, when Jesus said, "*As I have loved you, so you must love one another*" (John 13:34), Jesus was also pointing to *why* we must love one another. The Greek word that was translated as "as" in this verse also carries a causal meaning, so this verse could also be taken to mean "*because* I have loved you, so you must love one another." As John aptly summarizes in 1 John 4:19, "We love because He first loved us."

In Jesus's command, we are again seeing the linkage between our relationship with God and our relationship with others. It is precisely because we have received the extravagant gift of salvation, and it is precisely because our relationship with God has been restored, that we, in turn, must respond by loving one another with the love we have received. As discussed previously, our ability to live a life pleasing to God, which includes our ability to love one another in Jesus's community, stems from our restored relationship with God. We will only be able to love one another by being rooted in His love, abiding in Him like branches to the vine, as we learn to love each other with the endless supply of love from our trinitarian God. We have been given the Holy Spirit, who dwells in us to help us obey Jesus's command, and when we do, we will abide further in the love of Jesus. It is a beautiful picture where through our intimate abiding with the Holy Trinity, the love we have received will overflow to enable us to love one another. We will learn to love with the love God has loved us with, and in the way God has loved us.

6. THERE IS ONLY ONE COMMUNITY

We are sent into the world as one community to witness and continue Christ's work

Few would deny that Jesus's command to love one another is important. After all, God is love. If we are to be His followers and we are told to emulate Jesus, Jesus's command for us to love one another is hardly unexpected. But we must note that with this command, Jesus was specifically calling us to love those *within His Church*, thus revealing that there is something uniquely important about our relationship with fellow believers. Jesus Himself provided an explanation for this command in John 13:35, "By this everyone will know that you are my disciples, if you love one another."

The phrase "everyone will know" reminds us that beyond our community, the world is observing us. How we, as Jesus's disciples, carry ourselves as a group matters, because the world is looking at us, trying to understand who Jesus is and what is special about this group of followers. This is why loving one another within Jesus's community is a tell-tale sign of our identity as Jesus's disciples, because when we do that, we are reflecting who Jesus is with our actions. If God is love and Jesus was sent to die on the cross for humanity's sins out of love, how could Jesus's community, His disciples, not reflect this very nature of God within the body of Christ? When we love one another and be one and united in God's love, we reflect the unity and the fellowship of love that is shared among the Holy Trinity, as well as the fellowship we get to enjoy between God and ourselves, thereby living out our role as witnesses of Christ and His mission.

Indeed, we have a unique purpose as the Church. As the body of Christ, we are sent into the world to be Christ's witnesses to point people to Jesus and to continue doing His work with the help of the Holy Spirit (John 14:12; 15:27; 16:8–11; 17:18; 20:21). Jesus said in John 14:12, "Very truly I tell you, whoever believes in me will do the works I have been doing." But what is the work that Jesus did, the work we are supposed to continue? In Jesus's prayer to the Father before His departure in John 17, Jesus described the work He has finished as "I have revealed you (i.e., the Father) to those whom you gave me out of the world . . . and they have obeyed your word . . . For I gave them the words you gave me and they accepted them. They knew with certainty that I came from you, and they believed that you sent me" (John 17:6–8).

In these verses, Jesus was referring to the disciples who have accepted Christ as their Savior through faith and have since become members of God's kingdom. They have learned and accepted the word Jesus spoke to them, and have known God as the only true God who sent Jesus to die on the cross to bring salvation. From Jesus's own description, we can summarize His work as follows: to reveal who God is, to make known the relationship between Jesus and the Father, and to proclaim the good news, bringing salvation to all. This reminds us that everything Jesus did—whether it was His teaching, His miracles, or the healings He performed—they were all done to help us know God, to know that we have sinned and desperately need the salvation Jesus made available to us.

So what are we to do? Jesus said to the Father in John 17:18, "As you sent me into the world, I have sent them into the world." The analogy is unmistakable. We, the Church as one community, have been sent as Jesus was sent. Surely only Jesus's blood brings salvation, and there are aspects of Jesus's work that are beyond us because only Jesus is God. But we are to bear witness to God and reveal to the world who He is, and make known to the world the salvation that was achieved through Jesus by preaching the gospel, making disciples of all nations. It is demonstrating through our own lives what it means to honor and trust God now that our relationship with Him has been restored, to be set apart for God, and to be distinctively different as the salt and light of the world. As such, our mission to the world is an extension of our personal relationship with God, because when this relationship is reflected in our actions, people *will* see.

The interrelation between bearing witness as God's community and our personal relationship with God is further illustrated in John 15:8 (ESV). "By this my Father is glorified, that you bear much fruit and so prove to be my disciples." We might have thought of bearing witness as actions we do, which to a certain extent, it is. But this

6. THERE IS ONLY ONE COMMUNITY

verse reminds us that when we bear fruit as a natural outcome of abiding in Jesus, the fruit becomes outward proof of not only our restored relationship with God, but also our identity as members of God's kingdom. People will know that we belong to Jesus when we bear fruit, such as when we bear the fruit of the Holy Spirit by abiding in Jesus and allowing the Holy Spirit to lead our lives. "The fruit of the Spirit is love, joy, peace, forbearance, kindness, goodness, faithfulness, gentleness and self-control" (Gal. 5:22–23). When we remain in God, we will increasingly display characters that reflect God, such as His righteousness and goodness. This also includes our ability to love one another within the body of Christ, which grows as we are increasingly led by the Spirit in our everyday life. When we live a fruit-bearing life, we bring glory to God, just as Jesus brought the Father glory on earth by completing the work the Father sent Him to do (John 17:4).

Everything we have discussed above probably sounds really familiar—preaching the gospel, bearing fruit for God, and learning to love on this lifelong path of sanctification. Yet, if we are not careful, we could miss the big picture of Jesus's true vision for His community. In Jesus's final prayer before His departure, when He was laying before the Father His cares and concerns for this community He was leaving behind, what did He pray for? He asked the Father to protect the believers from evil (John 17:15). He asked the Father to sanctify them by the truth (John 17:17). But the one thing Jesus repeatedly asked for was *the unity of the believers*. Jesus prayed in John 17:11 for His disciples, "so that they may be one as we are one." This request was later repeated (John 17:20–21), but this time for all believers, including those who will believe through the disciples' message, "that all of them may be one, Father, just as you are in me and I am in you." Jesus was even going to give the glory which the Father has given Him to the believers, His Church, "that they may be one even as we are one, I in them and you in me, that they may become perfectly one" (John 17:22–23 ESV). This means that in the span of three verses, the word "one" has been used four times.

Why was Jesus so concerned with the unity of all believers? He provided the explanation Himself, "so that the world may know that you sent me and loved them even as you loved me" (John 17:23 ESV). It was so important to Him that the first part of the reason was stated twice (John 17:21, 23). Jesus knew. He knows that when we are all fired up in our love for Him, we will preach the gospel, we will have tremendous love for all the lost sheep, and we will have faith to do many spectacular things for Him. *Yet we may not love one another. We may not be united.* Jesus does not just want us to live our lives for Him; He wants us to live our lives for Him *together*, as *one community*, because our unity is how people will believe that the Father has indeed sent His son to die for us out of love. We need to reflect God's character, the oneness, the love; we need to reflect the fellowship within the Holy Trinity that is now also happening in our lives because of our restored relationship with God. We need to walk the talk, bearing fruit as one body and not just as individuals, because this is how they will know that our God is the living God. That is the most powerful testimony we can bear for Jesus, and it is something that deserves our focused attention and effort.

We need each other in this community that is in the world but does not belong to the world

But there is still another reason why unity in the Church and whether we love one another is important, and why this was so much on Jesus's mind before His departure. In John 15, right after Jesus told His disciples about the analogy of the vine and urged them to love one another, He proceeded to disclose the challenges they would face after Jesus returned to the Father. Jesus said in John 15:18–19, "If the world hates you, keep in mind that it hated me first. If you belonged to the world, it would love you as its own. As it is, you do not belong to the world, but I have chosen you out of the world. That is why the world hates you."

Jesus made it clear that those who persecuted Jesus would also persecute His Church. We who bear His name, who are called to be distinctively different, will be treated the same way He was treated. According to the world, we who belong to Jesus are one community,

6. THERE IS ONLY ONE COMMUNITY

regardless of our individual differences—and we face a hostile world, because "light has come into the world, but people loved darkness instead of light because their deeds were evil" (John 3:19). Paul reminds us that the enemy we are facing, the source of evil that enshrouds the world, "is not against flesh and blood, but against the rulers, against the authorities, against the powers of this dark world and against the spiritual forces of evil in the heavenly realms" (Eph. 6:12). It is capable of presenting itself in various forms of challenges, such as in the form of false teachers, heretic doctrines, persecutions or cultural trends and theories that run counter to the truth of Christ.

Jesus knew it would be a precarious situation. The disciples would suddenly find themselves without their mentor and their Lord. They would have a hard time comprehending the death and resurrection of Jesus, and the persecution that followed. This is why Jesus repeatedly encouraged the disciples to not let their hearts be troubled and to not be afraid, telling them that He was leaving His peace with them (John 14:1, 27; 16:33). He promised the disciples that He would ask the Father to send the Holy Spirit, and He prayed for the Father to protect them from the evil one (John 14:26; 16:7–15; 17:11, 15).

Jesus knew something that we often forget: we are vulnerable. We are mere creatures and our flesh is strong, but we are in battle. We need God the Father, we need Jesus, we need the Holy Spirit, and we need each other during our journey on earth. As relational beings created in God's image, we need our companions, our fellow brothers and sisters. Furthermore, we need to build up the body of Christ so that as a united community, we can stand firm. "Though one may be overpowered, two can defend themselves. A cord of three strands is not quickly broken" (Eccl. 4:12). The various spiritual gifts given to us were given so that the Church can grow and mature and be edified. This way, we will no longer be "tossed back and forth by the waves, and blown here and there by every wind of teaching and by the cunning and craftiness of people in their deceitful schemes" (Eph. 4:14). This is why it is so crucial that we are united, that we love one another, because it is only when we are joined together and growing into the holy temple in the Lord that we will be able to withstand the challenges coming our way.

Jesus Himself has stated in Matthew 12:25, "Every city or household divided against itself will not stand." Sadly, we are all aware of how difficult unity is and how divided the Church has been. The reality reminds us that it has indeed been the grace of God that the Church has remained standing through the centuries. As much as the Church is made of believers who are merely humans, it is in the world but not of this world because we have Christ as our head. But precisely because it is God's grace that has been carrying us this whole time, we must not lose sight of God's original intent for His community. In the next chapter, we will take a closer look at the challenges we face in our relationships with brothers and sisters as we strive to be united in God's love, and what are some ways we can tackle these challenges.

Points for Reflection

1. Are you surprised that being part of God's Church is inevitable for all believers based on God's design and His will? Does this change your perspective regarding your Christian community? If yes, what are your new realizations?
2. We have often downplayed the importance of loving one another and our unity as one Church in our walk with God. Why do you think this is the case? Do you personally struggle with this idea? In your quiet time, ask God to reveal to you the fears and doubts that may have caused you to downplay this aspect of your faith, and write them down in your journal.

7. APPLICATION: LIVING AS ONE COMMUNITY
REFLECTING ON THE CHALLENGES WE FACE AND WHAT TO DO ABOUT THEM

Reflection Questions

1. What challenges do you face when interacting with brothers and sisters?
2. How have you dealt with the disappointments you may have experienced in your Christian community?

For some believers, the previous chapter could be puzzling because our own experiences with Christian communities are often not quite as described. We understand that there is supposedly only one community, the body of Christ; yet, not only is the world populated with millions of churches of different denominations and statements of faith, but many cannot seem to see eye to eye on a myriad of doctrinal and theological issues. We know we are meant to be united and loving one another, but often we struggle to even get along with believers in our own communities. We are envious of the early Church—the way they were one in heart and mind, gathering daily to praise God and enjoying each other's fellowship, readily selling their possessions to give to anyone in need (Acts 2:44–47; 4:32–35). But we are also so used to seeing and experiencing the watered-down version of church life that we do not bat an eye anymore at conflicts and dissensions, or people leaving our communities. Consequently, we read these passages as unreachable ideals, treating them as ancient history that is no longer relevant to our current communities.

When we revisit Jesus's vision for His Church, we cannot deny that the Church is not how Jesus intended it to be in more ways than one. Yet many of us have also experienced how difficult it is to live out Jesus's vision. We have all had our share of disappointments and disagreements within our Christian community. We had wanted to fellowship with brothers and sisters in love, but things often stopped being rosy after a little while. So we devote our energy to being better Christians, to preach the gospel, to take care of the poor, but all the while, we have also allowed our relationships with brothers and sisters to be in disrepair. Somewhere along the line, we have relegated this part of our faith, the part about community and loving one another and being united, to the sideline. It is heartbreaking to see how fervently Jesus prayed for the unity of His community before His departure, and yet our hearts have grown so callous toward the situation.

But there is still time. God is still waiting for us to grow and honor His commands for us to be united in love. Starting with ourselves, our relationship with each fellow believer and our own community, we can humbly seek God and ask Him to transform our minds and hearts. The Holy Spirit, who descended upon the early believers like tongues of fire in Acts 2, who enabled those early believers to be one in heart and mind, is still dwelling in us. Christ is still the head of the Church, and God is still protecting us from evil. If we will submit to God's will and obey, here is what Jesus has promised, "If you remain in me and my words remain in you, ask

7. APPLICATION: LIVING AS ONE COMMUNITY

whatever you wish, and it will be done for you" (John 15:7). God will make the impossible possible. Below we will first discuss how our mindset regarding church life and community can be expanded and renewed, followed by discussions on some of the ways we can address the challenges we face in living out the unity God intends for His children.

Recognizing the Inevitability of Connectedness

We need to be part of a local Christian community

The first concept that needs some realigning is the notion of one Church and one body of Christ. As briefly mentioned, it is confusing to see the large number of churches in the world when Jesus clearly stated that there is only one flock with Him as the shepherd. But when Jesus said that there is only one flock, He was not saying that there can only be one physical community that would be called His Church. The spread of Christianity is seen in the book of Acts alone: within a decade of Jesus's departure, there were already multiple local church communities, all worshipping God and acknowledging Jesus as the Messiah. But we are one Church because despite geographical and physical limitations, we believe in the same gospel, and we all honor Jesus as the head of the Church.

Undoubtedly, throughout the history of Christianity, there have been schisms and disputes of different sorts, which broke up the Church into various religious bodies and denominations. But the scripture reminds us that despite our differences, those who believe in the same Lord make one community, because "there is one body and one Spirit . . . one Lord, one faith, one baptism; one God and Father of all" (Eph. 4:4–6). When Jesus said that we should be united as one, He was commanding us to look past our differences and recognize that we have been one body after all. We are all connected to Jesus, the one true vine; the connectedness is inevitable.

Then what is the significance of being part of a local Christian community? If we are each connected to Jesus through our personal faith, aren't we already one with billions of believers without having to meet them? How, then, should we understand Jesus's command to be one with other believers on an individual level? The most important thing to note is that Jesus was not only telling us that we are one community—but we are one community within which we are to *love and serve one another*, and work together to build up the body of Christ.

Therefore to live out this identity, we need to belong to a local Christian community, because there is no loving one another if we do not even have a relationship with other believers. It is within this community that we practice honoring God's call to be one in heart and mind, learning to love one another, and recognizing that regardless of how we feel about those in our community, we indeed belong to the same body of Christ. We simply cannot be faithfully following Jesus without committing to a body of believers through faith, engaging with them, and fellowshipping with them. Being a part of a local Christian community is thus essential for our faith.

We need each other as limited and dependent creatures

But there are more facets to the necessity of a community. Beyond the fact that we are commanded to be one community, God as our Maker knows *we need each other* because of the very nature of our being. As discussed, we as creatures are limited and dependent by nature. Therefore we are dependent on God (for His provision, sustenance, protection, etc.), but also on each other. This fact seems contradictory to what our world is telling us. With the advance in technology, we have seemingly grown to be much more capable of independence and autonomy, instead of relying on others. Yet underneath that façade of self-sufficiency, we need other humans and have been depending on them whether we acknowledge it or not. From infancy to adulthood, we have relied on many others for sustenance and livelihood, whether it is someone close to us, like our family, or others more distant such as planners and workers who give us roads, water, and electricity. Away from the Garden of Eden,

7. APPLICATION: LIVING AS ONE COMMUNITY

God has often provided for us and protected us through other human beings. We are made to depend on each other because in God's original design, not one of us can do everything in our limited, fleshly nature.

Likewise, we must depend on and work with each other to live out God's calling for the Church. It is a mission meant for a team, a community. For example, none of us can spread the gospel to the entire world through our own effort. In fact, we are all granted different spiritual gifts by the Holy Spirit for the common good, so that we can each be a functional part of the body of Christ (1 Cor. 12:7). We are to be joined together through love, working together, serving and honoring each other, so to edify and build up the Church. This is how we will be able to bear witness for Christ and the good news as one united body.

Therefore, nobody can say we do not need the other parts because each one is necessary and has a role to play, even though in our creaturely minds, we think some gifts are more important and better than others. To this misconception, Paul lays it out plainly in 1 Cor. 12:21–22, "The eye cannot say to the hand, 'I don't need you!' And the head cannot say to the feet, 'I don't need you!' On the contrary, those parts of the body that seem to be weaker are indispensable." At a time when we so often grumble and complain about other believers when we serve together, especially regarding those we disagree with, this reminder never gets old.

We need a community because we are made to fellowship

Furthermore, being made in the image of God means that we are relational by nature because our God is relational. Therefore, our need for relationships and fellowships is fundamental to our being, not optional. Beyond our dependence on each other because of our limited, fleshly nature, we are made with a desire and a need to relate to another being. Of course, first and foremost, we are made to fellowship with our heavenly Father. But when God said, "It is not good for the man to be alone" (Gen. 2:18), and subsequently created woman to be the man's helper, He was also speaking of our need to relate and fellowship with other human beings. We, by nature, need human interactions; we long to connect, to be understood, and to feel like we belong. It brings so much joy and fulfillment to know that others share our experiences, and for many of us, relationships are what bring meaning to life. It is a need beyond personality differences, a need central to our being, and a need that we must recognize.

God knows full well our need for companionship and this sense of solidarity with others. Therefore in His design, we are meant to have companions as we embark on our new lives as God's children. Learning to grow and mature as a follower of Christ is, after all, a life-long journey with challenges and ups and downs. The constant pull of the world and our old self is very real because we are in constant battle with our sinful nature and the forces of evil in this sinful world. This is why God gives us companions, our fellow believers, because we need encouragement and reinforcement to know that we can continue this journey even when it gets difficult. We need companions who understand our wrestle with our old selves, and someone to remind us to seek God when negativity runs amok and takes control of our lives. We need someone who can pray for and with us, someone to support us and spur us on when we feel downhearted and exhausted.

On the other hand, nothing reinforces our identity as members of God's kingdom like when believers gather together. Have you ever been filled with this tingling excitement of being in a house full of believers, all singing praises and crying out to God in unity? Or when everyone is bowing their heads in murmurs of prayers? These experiences and the Holy Communion we share bring home the reality that we are indeed one, that we are each connected to our Father and with each other. We need these experiences, these actual interactions with fellow believers, to fully grasp what it means to have been redeemed into the Church of God.

In addition, often it is through these interactions, whether negative or positive, that we finally understand many teachings in the Bible in a substantial way. It is only when we put into practice what we have learned through interacting with brothers and sisters

7. APPLICATION: LIVING AS ONE COMMUNITY

that we come to see what it means to relate, to fellowship, to love, to share, and to forgive. Sometimes these experiences, in turn, grant us a new understanding of how we should relate to our heavenly Father, because as much as our relationship with God is already restored, it can be challenging learning to fellowship with a God we cannot see.

So what does recognizing that we are relational in nature mean for our church life? It reminds us that while not all of us are naturally inclined toward the idea of community and fellowship, it is much more fundamental to our being than most have assumed. This explains the joy we experience when we find our Christian communities, because it addresses our fundamental need to feel accepted and to feel that we belong. Unfortunately, this has not been our experience at church for some of us. Many have turned away from church because they feel hurt or ignored, or when they cannot find that sense of belonging in the community. But the relational nature of our being reminds us that we do need each other, after all, even when we think that we can turn our back on the notion of community. Navigating through our relationships at church is something worthy of our effort and prayers, because this is in accordance with God's perfect plan.

Letting God be the center of our relationships

YET ACCEPTING our relational nature only brings another question. If we are made to fellowship, why is it so difficult to fellowship with other believers and be united as one community, as Jesus has intended? Why aren't we getting along swimmingly without even trying? To answer these questions, we need to recognize an inherent challenge we face when we try to fellowship with others, one that entered our lives during the Fall of mankind. In Ch.3, we talk about how Adam and Eve's decision to disobey God resulted in the disintegration of mankind's relationship with our heavenly Father. Sadly, accompanying our broken relationship with God are two things that also hinder our relationship with others.

First, with the Fall, mankind is filled with a tremendous sense of shame and insecurity. Like when Adam and Eve tried to hide from God after the Fall, we often feel incredibly uncomfortable exposing our true selves to others. This interferes with our ability to relate to others in a truthful and in-depth manner. As a result, we have a convoluted love-hate relationship with the notion of relationship itself. We are made with a desire to relate and bond, yet we are fearful and avoidant. Second, because the primal sin is associated with the desire to *become* God, we fall prey to self-centeredness and pride in our fallen state. Unfortunately, when we are unaware of how pride and self-centeredness still dominate our interactions with others, these sins lead to disagreements, conflicts, and disappointments in our relationships.

When we understand the way sins affect our relationships with others, we will see the unique challenge that comes with God's command for us to love one another and be united. Indeed, if the building unit of a God-centered community involves two redeemed sinners who are insecure, prideful, and self-centered, both merely learning to love in God's way instead of our natural, fleshly way, then it is obvious that God is desperately needed in every aspect of our relationships. In fact, we need God at the *center* of all our relationships, instead of letting Him be an afterthought or our contingency plan. We need to actively pray and seek God and His grace every step of the way in our interactions, so that we can love with His love like branches abiding in the vine, thereby letting His guidance and healing transform our community. It is an endeavor that has no room for spectators or consumers, because a loving and united community can only be achieved if we *all* draw on the grace and love of God to build up His community through our obedience. In the remainder of this chapter, we will focus on several aspects of our interactions that can be transformed by God's love and grace, so that people will know that we are Jesus's disciples by the love we share.

7. APPLICATION: LIVING AS ONE COMMUNITY

Surrender our insecurities, pride, and self-centeredness to the Lord

One thing that may be surprising to most people is that in order to love one another as God commanded, a big part of it is allowing God to work on our hearts and transform us through our personal relationship with Him. In particular, we need the Holy Spirit to help us surrender our self-centeredness, pride, and insecurities into His hands so that we can be set free from these struggles—footholds that the devil takes advantage of repeatedly to create dissensions in church. The scripture is full of reminders urging us to beware of various manifestations of these struggles. For example, in Paul's call for the Philippian believers to be united, he said in Phil. 2:3, "Do nothing out of selfish ambition or vain conceit. Rather, in humility value others above yourselves." In this verse, Paul points out two things that would get in the way of unity and us loving one another: selfish ambition and vain conceit. But what does Paul mean by these terms, and why are they so common that Paul would need to warn us against these attitudes?

The term "selfish ambition" refers to an attitude that is competitive, self-seeking, and interested in gaining an advantage over others.[1] It is an attitude that stems from self-centeredness as it is predominantly concerned with personal gain, and a competitive spirit longing to excel and be validated. While excellence and ambition are lauded as virtues in our modern society, danger lurks behind a selfishly ambitious mindset as it stirs up pride and prompts us to compare. Underlying the desire to achieve and be validated is often a self-directed need to ease our deeply-hidden insecurities and a sense of inadequacy when our value is not rooted in God's love. As a result, we compare and compete, hoping to seek outside proof of our worthiness. But when self-centeredness and insecurities dictate our interactions, what results is an individualistic, rival spirit, instead of one focused on community and fellowship. Therefore before we can be united, selfish ambition is a temptation and danger that we each must acknowledge and guard against.

The term "vain conceit," on the other hand, refers to vanity and pride that is groundless.[2] It speaks of the kind of pride that is not grounded in truth, like when creatures refuse to acknowledge our roles but tries to take the place of the Creator. An example would be when we try to be our master instead of honoring God as Lord. It is an inflated fixation on our achievements that blinds us from seeing God's grace and the contribution of others. Consequently, we think of ourselves more highly than we ought, overestimating our importance and contribution to the body of Christ (Rom. 12:3), which then tempts us to be boastful toward our fellow believers. Indeed, we are urged repeatedly in the scripture to not be prideful or arrogant when it comes to our relationship with brothers and sisters (Rom. 12:16; Gal. 5:26; James 3:14), because it would only disrupt fellowship and hinder unity. Thus with two terms, Paul reveals the presence of self-centeredness, pride, and insecurities in these toxic attitudes that make fellowship, loving relationships, and unity difficult in our Christian community. They are ubiquitous because they are inherent in our sinful nature.

But Paul does not stop there in his call for unity. He next exhorts us to be humble and consider others more significant than ourselves, looking out for their interests (Phil. 2:3–4). In Greek, "humility" is defined as an attitude of lowliness instead of a projection of self-importance, and the quality of voluntary submission and unselfishness.[3] From this definition, we see that humility is beyond modesty on an individual level, but it has an interpersonal component where one is willing to yield in selflessness. This shows us why humility is essential for unity and why unity is an impossible goal if we are left on our own to achieve it. We need the Holy Spirit to help us overcome our tendencies for selfish ambition and vain conceit, and to remind us of God's love to cast away our insecurity, so that we can adopt an attitude of lowliness and humility.

Indeed, true humility comes only with a healthy self-image rooted in the truth of God and His grace. It is remembering that we are mere creatures and not the Creator, yet despite our frail and limited nature, there is no need to feel ashamed because we are loved and considered worthy by our heavenly Father. It is knowing that even when we consider others more significant than ourselves,

7. APPLICATION: LIVING AS ONE COMMUNITY

we are still worthy and precious. We do not need to assert our importance or our right because God defines our worth. It is recognizing that as we voluntarily submit to the needs of others in obedience to God, our faithful God who loves us tremendously will watch over us and supply what we need. Jesus Himself has demonstrated what this looks like with His life. Fully aware of who He is, being fully God and thus equal with God the Father, He did not insist on His rights and position, but chose to voluntarily submit Himself in obedience to the Father's plan for Him on earth (Phil. 2:6–8). Through the power of the Holy Spirit, we, too, can choose to lay down our personal rights or interests to honor the needs and interests of others above our own.

So how do we know whether our identity is rooted in the Lord? How do we know if we are suffering from selfish ambition and vain conceit, or if we are acting with humility? Paul's command reminds us that while a life pleasing to God includes actions that are done according to God's will, the *attitudes and motives* with which we do these actions are equally important. Yet, our motives and attitudes are hidden from everyone else, and our true intentions can only be known between ourselves and the Lord. We must therefore learn to cultivate a healthy sense of self-awareness through honest, prayerful introspection in the Lord, asking the Holy Spirit to reveal to us what is in our hearts, so that we won't sin against God by acting with impure motives. This is how our hearts, emotions, and minds are surrendered to God and His transforming love, so that our motives and attitudes, together with our actions, are led by the Spirit instead of the flesh.

Accepting one another—a community that is hospitable and inclusive

Now that we have addressed the temptations that hinder our ability to love one another and be united, we are ready to ask: what does a community characterized by the love of Christ look like? In what ways should we be different from other social organizations so that we can be the pleasing aroma of Christ in a world that does not know God? In today's society, where people are marginalized and excluded for various reasons, where many social entities are characterized by cliques and selectivity, a telltale sign that Christ's community is distinct is a spirit of inclusion and hospitality. Paul says in Rom. 15:7, "Accept one another, then, just as Christ accepted you, in order to bring praise to God." We are called to accept, welcome, and receive one another hospitably,[4] regardless of our backgrounds, ethnicities, and social status. This is because not only has Christ died for everybody and made salvation available to all, but those of us who have accepted Christ are united by the same Lord, Father, and Spirit. Inherent in this command is the idea that everyone should be treated equally, with the same kindness, the same level of acceptance, and the same sincere love, because this is how Christ has accepted us.

This is a command most of us are familiar with, but there is more to this command when we delve deeper into it. Is this command a reminder that we should be friendly and welcoming to new friends in our congregations and our lives? Yes, we are called to pursue hospitality, which is mainly concerning visitors and strangers.[5] But we are also called to accept and welcome everyone in our congregation with the same level of acceptance—then it is not always easy. Many of us can be hospitable and welcoming to new people who visit our communities, but with time, differences in our personalities or opinions may cause us to leave certain people within our congregation behind. This is because we are naturally selective and limited in our love for others in our sinful, fleshly selves. We prefer those we find compatible or those similar to ourselves in terms of background and value.

But God is commanding us to accept each other just as Christ accepted us. And how has Jesus accepted us? Out of a tremendous love that considers everyone worthy, precious, and deserving of His gift of salvation. Therefore we try to be kind and inclusive, because we recognize that everyone we come across is someone Jesus died for, and we have been united with our brothers and sisters as one because of Jesus's blood. We accept each other out of love because we acknowledge that this is how Jesus loves all of us, and this is how

7. APPLICATION: LIVING AS ONE COMMUNITY

Jesus wants us to love one another. Consequently, we are welcoming and accepting not because we want to satisfy our self-serving intention to appear as good Christians or to win love and approval from others. Instead, we love and accept others, even if it means laying aside our personal preferences, because we value others above ourselves and recognize that in the love of Christ, no one should feel or be excluded.

Paul reminds us, "Love must be free of hypocrisy" (Rom. 12:9 NASB). Following the command to accept one another does not mean we have to pretend to be best friends with everybody. But it does mean that we each be more conscious in seeking God and His grace to become more accepting and hospitable. It means choosing to love everyone in the congregation with openness and a willingness to know and connect with every fellow believer, learning to accept and respect our differences. It means keeping our cliquish tendency in check and being mindful of whether we are welcoming and inclusive in our interactions. It also means considering everyone worthy enough of our care, encouragement, prayers, and help, despite our many differences. Finally, it is prayerfully asking God to help us maintain the perspective that everyone in the community is precious and deeply loved by Jesus, so that we learn to honor and accept them the way Jesus would. This is how God's community will be distinct from other communities, and how we bring glory to God.

Bearing with one another as fellow redeemed sinners

But learning to accept one another is only the beginning of a loving community. As fellow members of God's kingdom, we are also called to bear with one another (Eph. 4:2; Col. 3:13). In Greek, the verb "bear with" means "endure, exercising self-restraint and tolerance"; or "putting up with it when faced with something that is disagreeable, annoying or difficult."[6] At the core of this command is the acknowledgment that the people we are commanded to love can appear unreasonable, annoying, and even disappointing. Indeed, any of us who have been in a community for a while will probably agree that there is always someone who gets on our nerves. Yet with this command, God is not only forewarning us that there will be people whom we will have a hard time loving, but He is asking us to love these people anyway by bearing with them, putting up with them by exercising self-restraint.

God is asking us to act in a way that is opposite from what we would typically do—we are used to loving those who love us, in the way we have been loved. But if we rely on our fellow believers to supply us with the love and motivation we need to love them back, we will only be disappointed in the long run. Rather, God is asking us not to benchmark our love for other believers based on how they have treated us, but on how *God has treated us* and how *God would like us to treat them*. Our God has chosen to love us even when we were His enemies, despite being fully aware of our sinful and fickle nature. He bears with us even when we continue to sin against Him day after day. So here God is calling us to love and bear with our fellow believers with the love we have received from our heavenly Father, recognizing that this is how He bears with each of us too.

In fact, what God asks of us is precisely what Paul urges us to do in Eph. 4:22–24—to put off our old selves and put on our new selves. We are to shed our old, fleshly way of loving one another and put on God's new way. This is only possible with God's grace and the help of the Holy Spirit, as we learn to put away our self-centeredness and pride, and exercise self-restraint and bear with others.

When we grow in our ability to look away from our desires and rights in humility, we will realize another reason why we should bear with each other, and that is the fact that *we are all the same*. We are fellow redeemed sinners who may be different, but we all have the same desire to be loved and accepted, as well as the same struggles when it comes to learning to love and relate. We all struggle with insecurity and pride, and we are all still learning to follow the Spirit instead of our flesh. We might think that the problems in our relationships are because others are too difficult, but maybe what we experience is simply two fleshly, limited sinners with different personalities and upbringings trying to fellowship together. Thus when God asks us to bear with one another, He is asking us to

7. APPLICATION: LIVING AS ONE COMMUNITY

understand and empathize instead of taking offense and reacting based on our flesh. Our fellow believers are someone we can empathize with because we are all fallen creatures who have received the grace of God. Let us *be* the ones who break our fleshly pattern of interaction by choosing to bear with each other, and with God's help, we can.

Learning to be companions on our heavenward journey

Coming to terms with the fact that we all struggle brings forth another beautiful truth in God's perfect plan. Precisely because we share the same struggles, we are each other's perfect companions on our heavenward journey. As discussed, we all need companions on our journey on earth. None of us can always be strong, regardless of how we look on the outside, because we all experience ups and downs in our spiritual life. Therefore, as part of God's community, we must take turns to be the positive influence and encourage each other, because none of us can do it all. Gal. 6:2 reminds us, "Carry each other's burdens, and in this way you will fulfill the law of Christ."

Some of us may feel that we are too weak and too green in our faith to be a positive influence. Yet what enables us to carry others' burdens is the Holy Spirit that dwells in each of us. Through Him, we can each channel the love and mercy of God, and be the source of grace and encouragement others may need. Furthermore, being a companion in God's community is never about being able to provide solutions for people's problems, or leading them out of the darkness they are experiencing. We have God for that, who is wise, mighty, and loves us unconditionally. As companions, we only have to *be there*, to walk together, to pray together, to "rejoice with those who rejoice; mourn with those who mourn" (Rom. 12:15), as we take turns encouraging each other to seek God together.

Nonetheless, to embark on this journey of fellowship, we must guard our hearts against the usual culprits of pride and insecurities, for nothing destroys our relationships like these dark tendencies in our hearts. Our pride and self-centeredness fool us into thinking that fellowship and companionship are unnecessary, and our insecurities prevent us from opening up and honestly sharing our struggles with others. Yet all of us need the support and comfort of our fellow believers, regardless of how mature we believe we are in the Lord. Therefore we must form the habit of cultivating more in-depth relationships with other believers, people with whom we can pray and seek the Lord together.[7] Let our identity be rooted constantly in the truth of God, so that we remember that we are limited and sin-laden, but also loved and accepted, with God providing us with everything we need on our heavenward journey. When we continue to journey together and learn to draw on God's strength together, our steadfast acts of kindness and companionship will allow us to experience the true meaning of fellowship and companionship. This is the beauty and intimacy inherent in God's perfect design of a loving and united community.

Building each other up in the Church of God

If the Church is to be a community characterized by love, humility, and servanthood, then there is nothing that helps us understand the notion of serving one another more than God's call for us to build each other up in His community. Paul mentions in 1 Cor. 12:7 that we are each given gifts of the Spirit "for the common good." Peter reaffirms this message in 1 Pet. 4:10 by stating, "Each of you should use whatever gift you have received to serve others, as faithful stewards of God's grace in its various forms."

These verses draw our attention to two important observations. First, whatever gifts we have are *given* to us by the Holy Spirit. We have done nothing to earn them; hence we have no reason to boast. Second, we do not know why we are each given the gifts we have, nor do we know why some people have more gifts than others. But the reason why we are given gifts are clearly stated, and that is to serve each other. We are to be conduits of God's grace "so that the body of Christ may be built up" (Eph. 4:12). It reminds us that the objective of our service is God-directed and others-directed, instead of self-directed. Inherent in the idea of spiritual gifts is the notion

7. APPLICATION: LIVING AS ONE COMMUNITY

that God's community is built up first and foremost by God's grace, because these gifts are given to us who are limited and dependent, and yet when we serve each other with these gifts, the body of Christ is built up. In addition, the fact that different gifts are given to everyone, meaning not one person has all the gifts, highlights the essentiality of every member of the community and the importance of unity. Indeed, it is only when we are united in our objective of serving each other and building up the Church that we can properly execute God's plan for His community.

But learning to view and exercise our spiritual gifts with a godly attitude can be tricky. The nature of spiritual gifts can lead to many comparisons, and it is a spawning ground for pride and insecurities. Comparisons can happen on many levels, from whether certain gifts are better than others, to the number of gifts any individual is blessed with, or whether someone is more gifted between two individuals with the same gift. We are called to serve each other, but right when we engage in actual service, our hearts become a battlefield. We are forced to come face to face with our insecurities when we feel that we have been given gifts that are less visible or less important, or when we feel like we are less gifted compared to others. Conversely, we can be swamped with a sense of superiority and pride when we think we are "better" than our brothers and sisters. Sometimes we are also tempted to gauge the efficacy of our services based on people's feedback and approval, which in turn serve as tools for us to bolster or cast doubts on our self-esteem.

And in the midst of it all, we forget that it was never about ourselves. We forget that gifts are not given to prove our worthiness. We are already loved, already worthy, because God says so. We do not need to put up a fight to demonstrate that we deserve to be part of the community. God has already included us in His plan, and we each have a specific role. On the other hand, the gifts are also not given to us as tools to build our legacy or purely for our self-actualization, because the community is, after all, built by God's grace and for His glory.

Therefore, in this constant roller-coaster of our self-image, we must anchor our service once again in God's love in our personal relationship with Him, and keep our eyes on the one who called us to serve. He is only asking us to be faithful with what He has entrusted to us, and when we do, we are treated to a front-row seat to witness God's awe-inspiring power. We will witness His loving faithfulness as His plan unfolds, and we will come to appreciate what a privilege it is to serve with our gifts because it is working together with God. Furthermore, we will be reminded that the purpose of our gifts is to serve God and our fellow believers, instead of ourselves.

This is why Paul says in 1 Cor. 12:31, after he has listed the many gifts given to believers, "and yet I will show you the most excellent way." What is the most excellent way? It is the way of love, as documented in the famous 1 Corinthians 13. Because it is only in love, which enables us to be patient and kind, to delight in the truth, and not be proud or self-seeking, that we will be able to exercise our gifts the way God has intended—to love and serve each other, thereby building up the Church of God. Thus in everything we do, in all the ways we serve each other, let it be done out of love and humility for the benefit and edification of others. May God guard our hearts and give us wisdom so that our service indeed contributes to building up the Church of God for His glory.

Being a peacemaker in conflicts

Nonetheless, this chapter will not be complete without a more focused discussion of being a peacemaker in conflicts. Conflicts are unfortunately very common in Christian communities, but we are not very good at resolving them. The saddest thing about conflicts is that there are no winners; everyone is hurt, and every conflict becomes a foothold for the devil to drive a wedge between believers. The fact that both sides are angry and hurt in a conflict is probably also why so many conflicts are left unresolved. When both parties are waiting to be understood and comforted, the situation will only spiral downwards. But our God is the Lord of all our interactions, even our conflicts, and He Himself will provide us with everything we need to heal our relationships if we are willing.

7. APPLICATION: LIVING AS ONE COMMUNITY

Heb. 12:14 says, "Make every effort to live in peace with everyone and to be holy." The Holy Spirit is with us, and He will grant us the love, courage, and strength we need if we seek Him every step of the way.

So if we ever find ourselves in the middle of a conflict, how should we tackle it? When we feel wronged and angry and hurt, the first thing we need to address is our own anger and the temptation to retaliate. Paul reminds us in Eph. 4:26–27, "'In your anger do not sin': Do not let the sun go down while you are still angry, and do not give the devil a foothold." While our minds are likely racing to figure out who is right and who is wrong, what we must learn is to slow down and quiet down before God, and lift up our anger, frustrations and hurt into His hands in a timely manner. Let the love of God fill our hearts and remind us that we can rest in His love knowing that regardless of what has transpired, our God knows, and He is a just God who loves us. He understands how we feel, and there can be healing and comfort in Him.

Then, as our anger and hurt begin to subside, we must spend time in prayers to reflect on the situation, and hear what the Holy Spirit has to say. So often in conflicts, we are eager to insist on our perspectives and our way of doing things. But this is when we need to be reminded that our idea of right or wrong is often much more subjective than we think. In our fleshly selves, our views are limited, and none of us can judge what is truly good or right, because God alone holds this authority. When we humbly submit ourselves to God, we can prayerfully ask Him to grant us new insights and show us how we may look at the situation from His perspective. Maybe He will show us instances when we had reacted out of our pride or insecurities, and how we, despite feeling like we were the ones being attacked, also did our fair share of attacking.

If that is the case, may God grant us the courage and humility to seek His forgiveness, for we know that "He is faithful and just and will forgive us our sins and purify us from all unrighteousness" (1 John 1:9). On the other hand, maybe God will also grant us new understanding as to why our fellow brothers or sisters had reacted the way they did. Maybe God will shed light on the struggles they have been experiencing, sometimes through circumstances or even through other brothers and sisters.

Finally, if possible, pray for a good time to reach out and make peace. Find an opportunity to pray together, listen, share, and, where appropriate, apologize. Jesus made it clear in Matt. 5:23–24 that each of us has the responsibility to take the initiative to make peace urgently. "Therefore, if you are offering your gift at the altar and there remember that your brother or sister has something against you, leave your gift there in front of the altar. First go and be reconciled to them; then come and offer your gift." Jesus was asking us to go and be reconciled regardless of whose fault it was, even if it may be difficult and there is never any guarantee of the outcome. He was asking us to follow His way instead of our way, to be the one who seeks peace and healing because we know that the unity of the Church is more important than our personal strife. After all, what is there to insist on when we are all sinners forgiven at the cross of Jesus?

Eph. 4:32 reminds us, "Be kind and compassionate to one another, forgiving each another, just as in Christ God forgave you." We, too, can leave our grievances, hurt and disappointments at the cross and ask the Holy Spirit to give us the strength to forgive each other and choose peace. Despite our differences, we are all beloved children of our heavenly Father. Therefore let us choose to love so that Jesus's community will not be further torn apart. "Above all, love each other deeply, because love covers over a multitude of sins" (1 Pet. 4:8). When we follow God's command and choose peace with His strength, we can trust that God Himself will reward and also discipline those He loves. In His time, He will make everything beautiful again.

Remember this is God's Church—Never let people take God's place

Unfortunately, despite our best intention and effort to love and bear with one another with God's strength, our interactions with each other can still be plagued with disappointments. It can be

7. APPLICATION: LIVING AS ONE COMMUNITY

frustrating when our efforts have not seemingly made a difference in our relationships or the community. But in the grace of God, there are blessings even in disappointments. First, it reminds us that we and our fellow believers are indeed redeemed sinners who will continue to struggle with our fleshly selves. As much as we hope that church will be the place where we find love, justice, and truth, or that our fellow believers will be our most intimate companions on our heavenward journey, the truth is, we are all still learning to love and live a Spirit-led life. Even Peter the apostle, who once declared that he would lay down his life for Jesus, denied Jesus three times when danger befell him (John 13:37; 18:15–27). There will be times when we fail to love, and others fail to act with kindness.

Therefore, as much as we try to love one another, we must be careful to never let humans take the place of God. Our fellow believers might be our companions, our learning and sparring buddies, but they are never meant to be the *only* source of love, support, and approval. We must not place the hopes and trust meant for God in our fellow believers (including pastors), because when we do, they have inadvertently become idols in our lives. It is dangerous to let other believers take the place of God because any disappointments associated with them will cause us to lose hope in God, and may prompt us to leave the Church. Thus as we seek God's help with all our interactions, we must also keep in mind that God alone is the reason that we are in one community, and He alone is our Lord.

Second, disappointments remind us that we can only try our best in faithful obedience, but peace, reconciliation, and unity are in the hands and timing of God. It is a reminder to bring our focus back to God and remember that God has not stopped watching over His Church and His people, even if we might be overwhelmed in our efforts to love one another. Jesus is still the head of the Church, and this is His community. From God alone come all the grace, mercy, love, and strength that make the Church what it is—a group of redeemed sinners who serve as witnesses of God and His love, justice, and goodness. When we are reaffirmed that our effort to love one another stems from the recognition that His will for the Church is for us to be "like-minded, having the same love, being one in spirit and of one mind" (Phil. 2:2), we can trust that God sees our efforts despite our struggles and inadequacy.

Our God reigns, and He has sustained the Church through the centuries in His grace, mercy, and power. His will for His Church will prevail, and His victory is certain, as we will see in the next chapter. Our God has preserved His Church so people will recognize that He is God, and one day we will all share in His glory. When we keep our eyes on God and His kingdom, when we honor God's will for His community above all and wait upon His grace to carry us in our weaknesses, we will get to experience the unity and glory God intends for His people. We can place our hope on our glorious and victorious God.

> *Therefore, as God's chosen people, holy and dearly loved, clothe yourselves with compassion, kindness, humility, gentleness and patience. Bear with each other and forgive one another if any of you has a grievance against someone. Forgive as the Lord forgave you. And over all these virtues put on love, which binds them all together in perfect unity.*
>
> *Colossians 3:12–14*

Points for Reflection

1. When we recognize that humans are relational by nature, how does this change the way you understand and approach your relationship with brothers and sisters? Will you interact with them differently based on this newfound understanding?
2. Often, we are convinced that the disappointments and conflicts in our Christian communities are primarily due to others and their behaviors, without realizing that our insecurities and self-centeredness also contribute to the

7. APPLICATION: LIVING AS ONE COMMUNITY

issues. How does this realization affect the way you view the interpersonal struggles you face?

3. When was the last time you prayed specifically for your relationships at church, especially at times of disappointments and conflicts? Let us form the habits of praying for our interactions, and letting God be the center of our relationship and fellowship. Write in your journal one area in your relationships that needs God's grace and His help, and pray for God to bring healing, courage, and wisdom to know what can be done.

_____

8. THE BRIDE AWAITING HER GROOM
BEING GOD'S COMMUNITY ON EARTH IN ANTICIPATION OF JESUS'S RETURN

Reflection Questions

1. When the word "end time" is mentioned, what kind of images come to mind?
2. Do you look forward to heaven? How often do you think about the end time?

We have arrived at the last major topic of the book, and it is a full-circle moment. We started by realigning our perspectives on salvation, followed by an in-depth discussion of our restored relationship with God. We then shifted our discussion onto our relationships with others, focusing on God's calls for His Church to be a united community characterized by love and servanthood. We talked about our daily struggles with our sinful nature, and the

8. THE BRIDE AWAITING HER GROOM

importance of surrendering our will while learning to trust and rely on God completely. It is a balancing act that takes prayers, focus, introspection, and support from each other.

Yet while we are busy living the new life that comes with accepting Christ as our Savior, somehow we have slowly lost sight of the end time, even though for many of us, our awareness of this impending judgment was what brought us to Christ in the first place. Jesus is coming a second time, and with it comes a judgment and an end to this world as we know it. When it happens, everyone will have to answer for what we have done with our lives, and be separated into those who will be given eternal lives, and those heading to eternal destruction and separation from God. Yet, after we have been Christians for a while, the significance of eternity on our Christian walk is often lost amid our earthly striving. We forget that our time on earth is not meant to last forever. It is almost as if we feel like we are already saved, so the end time no longer matters.

But this awareness of the eschaton, the Greek equivalent of the word "last" that has come to refer to the end time, is essential, especially when we are trying to live a life pleasing to God. As an integral part of the gospel and Jesus's teaching, this is important not only in our personal relationship with God, but also for the Church as a community because the Church is to be the bride of Christ when He returns. The body of Christ is thus not just a collection of Christ's followers, but we are to be the bride who will be sanctified, holy and blameless, ready to be united to Christ during the wedding of the Lamb. This is an aspect of the Church's identity and mission on earth that was left out in the previous chapters, so its significance and implications can be explored in further detail here.

The beginning of the end—Jesus was raised from the dead

To understand the importance of the eschatological perspective in our faith, we need to return to the death and resurrection of Jesus Christ. Every Easter, we celebrate the resurrection of Jesus Christ to remember Jesus's victory over sin and death. The Son who was sent to die on the cross on our behalf, bearing the wages of our sins in the most excruciating death, was raised from the grave on the third day, victorious. We celebrate because the resurrection of Jesus Christ reminds us that death and sins are no match against our mighty God, and therefore we who are called His own can also be victorious and granted a way out of eternal death. There is much to celebrate, as we remember Jesus Christ as the Savior who has completed what He was sent to do, and is now seated at the right hand of God in glory.

But there is more to the significance and impact of Jesus's resurrection. In the gospels, Jesus repeatedly predicted His death and resurrection with His disciples (Matt. 16:21–23; 17:22–23; 20:17–19; Mark 8:31; 9:30–32; 10:33–34; Luke 9:21–22; 18:31–34), and yet the disciples never fully grasped what He meant. The disciples might have understood the part about Jesus being handed into the hands of men to be killed, which filled the disciples' hearts with grief and prompted Peter to exclaim, "Never, Lord!" (Matt. 16:22), but mostly the disciples failed to comprehend what Jesus said and were too afraid to ask (Matt. 16:21–23; 17:22–23; Mark 8:31–33; 9:30–32; Luke 9:43–35; 18:31–34).

When Jesus indeed died and was raised from the dead on the third day, it must have been exciting but also overwhelming and a little confusing, as the disciples looked back at the many things Jesus had taught them and slowly realized that *everything Jesus said was true*. Jesus did not just die on the cross; He was *raised on the third day*, as implausible as it seemed when Jesus made that declaration. They even witnessed the ascension of Jesus Christ, who returned to His Father in heaven as He said He would (John 16:28). Their beloved teacher was indeed the Son of God, who not only had the power to forgive sins and perform miracles, but He had conquered even death, the most daunting enemy of humanity and the one fate no one could escape, and emerged from it victorious and glorious.

This means that everything else Jesus talked about must also be true. Even if they had never seen heaven with their eyes and had yet to experience death themselves, when Jesus promised His disciples that He was going to His Father's house to prepare a place for them,

8. THE BRIDE AWAITING HER GROOM

they could trust that they would indeed be in the Father's house with Jesus one day (John 14:2–4).

Jesus's resurrection and ascension demonstrated that death is not the end of human's existence, nor is life on earth all that there is. It revealed that there can be life after death, and beyond the earth we call home, there is a heavenly home in another realm that Jesus has invited everyone to be a part of. Yet to be eligible for life in eternity, one needs to make the conscious choice to repent and believe in the Son of God during our very transient time on earth. This is because once our earthly lives come to an end, we would only be resurrected to eternal life or eternal destruction during the final judgment at the end time, when Jesus comes back for a second time (John 5:25–29). Implicit in Jesus's victory on the cross is another reality that is way more deserving of our attention, because it concerns eternity. The good news brought by Jesus, as the disciples would later realize, was not so much about the restoration of an earthly Israel kingdom, but it was about victory against death and evil in a realm unseen with our eyes. It is the establishment of a kingdom in eternity where God, who is seated on the throne, will spend eternity in loving fellowship with those who belong to Him in the new heaven and new earth.

This is the very reminder that is desperately needed today among followers of Christ—that beyond the world we can see and touch and feel is a realm unseen with our eyes, a realm that is extremely significant because it concerns our status in eternity. While this does not mean that our life on earth has lost all significance, it warns against focusing *only* on our earthly life. As Paul reminds us, "If only for this life we have hope in Christ, we are of all people most to be pitied" (1 Cor. 15:19). How, then, should we live with this renewed awareness of the eschaton, both in our individual relationship with God and as the community that bears Christ's name?

IN A RELATIONSHIP WITH GOD

The realm that is unseen

To answer this question, we need to gain a better understanding of what the heavenly realm is like, and what the eschaton will bring. Thankfully, God has chosen to reveal Himself and His plan through His word. In Revelation 4, we are treated to a glimpse of heaven in John's vision. In the vision, the first thing John noticed is a throne in heaven. Seated on the throne is God, who is described as having the appearance of jasper and ruby. Not only is there a rainbow that shines like an emerald encircling the throne, but in front of it are the seven spirits of God in the form of seven lamps and what looks like a sea of glass, clear as crystal. Flashes of lightning, rumblings, and peals of thunders come from the throne (Rev. 4:2–6).

It is an image that might be a little hard to imagine, but what it represents is clear. What we have is the image of the glory and honor of the Lord God Almighty seated on His throne. It reveals a God who is holy, powerful, and awe-inspiring, yet also faithful and merciful, as represented by the rainbow. It shows us that our God reigns, and He is to be praised and worshipped. Surrounding the throne are twenty-four thrones occupied by twenty-four elders wearing white garments and golden crowns, and four living creatures who worship and give glory, honor, and thanks to God day and night. It is non-stop worship of our God because He is worthy, as the Creator, and as the one "who was, who is, and is to come" (Rev. 4:6–11).

But the worship is not only directed at God who is on the throne. In the vision, they also worship the Lamb who was slain because with His blood, He "purchased for God persons from every tribe and language and people and nation." He also "made them a kingdom and priests to serve God" and will give them the privilege to reign on the earth (Rev. 5:9–10). In addition, they bow down before Jesus because He is the one who is worthy enough to take and open the scroll that is sealed with seven seals from the right hand of God. Once opened, the scroll will kickstart the events that bring the devil to its end and usher in the eternal reign of God in the new heaven and new earth. It is thus an over-

8. THE BRIDE AWAITING HER GROOM

flowing of endless praise, as countless angels and every creature join the elders and the living creatures to praise and worship Jesus and God who is on the throne (Rev. 5:11–13). It is a picture of joyous celebration because victory has already been won when the Lamb died on the cross, and history is ready to unfold, hurtling toward the renewal of creation when the new Jerusalem descends from heaven. The dwelling place of God will finally be with the people, and "He will dwell with them. They will be His people, and God Himself will be with them and be their God" (Rev. 21:2–3).

What Revelation 4–5 reveals is that our God has already won, and He is already on the throne. In fact, He has been on the throne this whole time. He reigns *now*, and we have already been purchased by the blood of Jesus, even though we are still engrossed in our daily struggles with sin and our old selves. This means that despite how things may look in our earthly realm, our heavenly Father and Creator, who loves us so deeply, is in control. He has not stopped watching over us. This is the second reminder we need as Christ's followers today, one that we need to encourage each other in our community to take to heart.

The end that is to come—the already but not yet

You may ask, if God already reigns, why are we still struggling? Why is our world still so broken and chaotic? To address this, we need to understand a term coined by theologians called "already but not yet," which refers to the interim between Jesus's first and second coming. It is "already" because Jesus has already died on the cross, and victory has already been won. It is "already" because the kingdom of God has been ushered in, and salvation has been made available to everyone through the blood of Jesus. But it is "not yet" because until Jesus returns to bring judgment on everyone and put an end to the devil for good, God's eternal reign and the full manifestation of His kingdom have "not yet" arrived. The renewal of creation, when God's redeemed people will be with Him forever and reign with Him in the new heaven and new earth, together with all the good things described in Rev. 21:1—22:5, are "not yet" a reality.

The interim is now. It is a time leading up to the end time, and it is a critical time, where a raging war unseen with our eyes is taking place. The interim is the window when every one of us is given a chance to accept the gospel and have our relationship with God restored during our time on earth. This is the time given to the world to respond through repentance and faith, because when Jesus comes back at the end time to judge everyone, it will be too late. It is during this interim that the Church of Jesus, those who belong to God, live out our identity as revealed by the heavenly chorus in Rev. 5:10—as the kingdom of priests to serve God. We are to be faithful witnesses of God and His gospel, bringing people to Christ by preaching the good news of Jesus, and making disciples of all nations.

It is almost paradoxical that our decisions and actions during our time on earth, which is extremely brief compared to eternity, will have eternal significance when the time of judgment arrives like a thief at an hour that no one will know (Matt. 24:36; Luke 12:40; 1 Thess 5:2; 2 Pet. 3:10). Yet the end point of those who pledge to follow Jesus until the end during this interim is clear. We are the ones who will have the seal of God on our foreheads, dressed in robes made white by the blood of the Lamb (Rev. 7:3, 14; 14:1). We are the ones whose names are written in the book of life during the final judgment because we belong to God, thus evading the second death by the lake of fire (Rev. 20:12, 15).

But the interim is also when the devil and his delegates are still roaming the world trying to "win" a battle they know they will definitely lose. We see through the visions of John what their ends will be; Satan and his minions, the beast and the false prophet, will all be thrown into the lake of burning sulfur (Rev. 19:20; 20:10). Yet precisely because they know their time is limited and their defeat is unavoidable, *in their desperation* they are determined to wreak havoc to the best of their ability before Jesus's return. If they are not going to win against God, they will target those they can accuse and deceive during the interim, the ones who are vulnerable—the people.

8. THE BRIDE AWAITING HER GROOM

The ongoing war is thus not so much against our mighty God, because the devil never stood a chance; it is a war for the souls of men. Pretending to be God and luring the world away from the truth of Christ through slander and deception, the devil builds his own following, those who would worship Babylon and all that it represents—the worship of sins, evilness, idols, success, and power, in rebellious independence from the living God. They are the ones who have the mark of the beast on their right hands or foreheads (Rev. 13:16), whose names are not in the book of life. They are the ones who refuse to repent and acknowledge that God is God, even as the clash between our Holy God and the sinful world intensifies, and we begin to see the wrath that comes with His holiness manifested with the imminent return of Jesus (Rev. 9:20–21; 16:9, 11). Unfortunately these are the ones who have chosen to pledge their allegiance to the devil, and they too, will share the same end as their master.

Yet the devil is not just targeting non-believers and keeping them from knowing or believing in Christ; he is determined to wage war on "those who keep God's commands and hold fast their testimony about Jesus" (Rev. 12:17; 13:7). The tricks devil uses to keep non-believers from following Christ is also used on believers to draw us away from God. We are told in Rev. 13:15–17 that the devil can cause those who refuse to worship the beast to be killed, or make it impossible for those without the mark of the beast to buy or sell. The devil is eager to fool us into thinking that following Jesus is *not worth it*, terrorizing us from continuing to follow Jesus.

But this is a blatant lie, because in John's visions, we see who truly reigns! Only our God is "the Alpha and the Omega, the First and the Last, the Beginning and the End" (Rev. 22:13). He alone is the one to be feared, the one who owns all power and authority, the one who provides and sustains. In addition, it is true that to live in a way pleasing to God is to live in a way that clashes with the values of the sinful world, and it has its costs. But these are temporary costs because the interim and our time on earth are extremely transient compared to eternity.

Revelation has made it amply clear that in the realm that is unseen with our eyes, when Jesus returns to judge the world, there are only two sides, two eternal outcomes. Either we are on God's side, or we are on the side of the devil. We are in the midst of war, the outcome of which has long been determined. The real danger is forgetting about this reality and forgetting that we are already on the winning side, so long as we continue to follow Jesus to the end and remain faithful to God amid the devil's increasingly desperate taunting (Rev. 13:10; 14:12). After all, we only triumph over the devil "by the blood of the Lamb and by the word of (our) testimony" (Rev. 12:11). Apart from Him, we are left vulnerable. This is why we must be alert and be of sober mind, and why we need to have the backs of our brothers and sisters and encourage each other to remain in the Lord, because "the devil prowls around like a roaring lion looking for someone to devour" (1 Pet. 5:8). This is our third reminder.

The Church being the bride to the Lamb

But what does it mean to remain faithful to God until the end? In the Bible, the relationship between God and His people has been likened to that of a marriage, with the Church described as a bride awaiting marriage to Jesus, the groom (Isa. 54:4–6; 61:10; Eph. 5:25–27; 2 Cor. 11:2). In John's vision, he witnessed the announcement that the wedding of the Lamb has finally arrived, "and his bride has made herself ready" (Rev. 19:7). The marriage analogy is a very rich imagery, and there is much that we can learn from it. But one thing that is undoubtedly illustrated, is that like a marriage agreement, what we have is a pledge, a covenant made with God when we each accepted Christ as our Savior—the pledge and covenant we must also honor as a community. Remaining faithful to God is thus remaining faithful to this pledge that we made on a personal and corporate level.

Yet before we discuss this in further detail, we need to first unpack the many insights from the marriage analogy to fully appreciate God's vision for His people at the end time. In Eph. 5:22–33, the Church is compared to the wife in a marriage, and is

8. THE BRIDE AWAITING HER GROOM

called to submit to Christ, who is the head of the Church. On the other hand, Christ loved the Church and gave Himself up for the Church, which we know refers to His sacrifice on the cross to grant us salvation. The comparison of our relationship with God to that of a husband and wife, first of all, reaffirms something we already talked about: at the crux of salvation is the restoration of our relationship with God. Similar to a marriage, this union is binding, and the nature of what has been restored is a relationship characterized by love, intimacy, and faithfulness.

Indeed, after Satan is defeated and the heaven and earth have been made new, at the center of the new creation is an eternal union and fellowship between God and His people. "Look! God's dwelling place is now among the people, and *He will dwell with them*. They will be His people, and God himself will be with them and be their God" (Rev. 21:3). A similar message is repeated in Rev. 21:7, with God declaring, "And I will be their God and they will be my children." These verses remind us that the best thing about heaven is that we will be with God forever, where the eternal relationship and fellowship with God is the very prize awarded to us. Our relationship with our heavenly Father will finally be restored to how it was in the Garden of Eden. The brokenness that entered our relationship with God and our lives will be undone along with the final victory. God will wipe every tear from our eyes, and there will be no more death, mourning, crying, or pain (Rev. 21:4).

A second aspect that is interesting about the marriage analogy is that the Church, not individual believers, is compared to the wife in a marriage. When the entire Church is referred to as the bride of Christ, we are reminded that even though we have often thought of our salvation as a personal decision, the community aspect of our salvation is just as important, if not more so. What was inaugurated with the work of Christ is a kingdom that, while made up of individuals, is one kingdom—a community that is united by the blood of Jesus, branches of the vine. There is only one Church, and everyone who belongs to Jesus is granted the same new identity as God's people. We see in John's vision that those who belong to God are the ones dressed in the same attire, white robes that have been washed and made white in the blood of the Lamb, even though they came from "every nation, tribe, people and language" (Rev. 6:11; 7:9, 13, 14). This signifies that while we all have different backgrounds and upbringings, once we accept Christ, our identity is first and foremost a member of God's kingdom, because this is the very identity that will determine our ending at the end time.

A bride that is holy and blameless

Nonetheless, as the bride of the Lamb, the Church has to be holy and blameless because Christ the groom is holy. The good news is that Christ made this possible with His own sacrifice. Eph. 5:25–27 (ESV) states that "Christ loved the Church and gave Himself up for her, that He might sanctify her, having cleansed her by the washing of water with the word, so that He might present the Church to Himself in splendor, without spot or wrinkle or any such thing, that she might be holy and without blemish." Christ did not just die for us to grant us eternal life through faith, but it is His will that the Church (and the individuals that make up the Church) be sanctified so that when Jesus returns, the Church can be presented to Himself as a holy and blameless bride.

But what does it mean to be holy and blameless? First, being holy means being set apart by God or for God.[1] The marriage analogy is tremendously helpful in illustrating this aspect of holiness. What often escapes our attention is that we, the Church, are in the middle of an engagement. The Church has *already* been betrothed to Christ, but the wedding feast has *not yet* happened (2 Cor. 11:2; Rev. 19:9). During this engagement period, we are to remain faithful to our future husband, Jesus Christ, set apart for Him alone.

This calls back to the question that was asked earlier and reveals that remaining faithful to God means being set apart for Him, in both our individual relationship with Him and as a community. It also helps us understand why unfaithfulness on our part, when we fail to worship God alone and continue to follow the sinful world, is such an abomination and upsets God. Imagine a fiancée who would go around pretending to be single and ready to get involved with

8. THE BRIDE AWAITING HER GROOM

anyone else. If this is upsetting and hurtful according to human standards, how much more would it grieve our holy God, and after He bought us at such a heavy price?

But there is also a second aspect to being holy and blameless: our righteous deeds as a community. The new heaven and new earth are where all evilness and unholiness are eradicated. "Nothing impure will ever enter it, nor will anyone who does what is shameful or deceitful, but only those whose names are written in the Lamb's book of life" (Rev. 21:27). Heaven is hardly heaven when people who do impure and unholy acts are allowed into it. The association of good deeds with being blameless is also seen in Rev. 19:7–8 (ESV). When it is time for the wedding of the Lamb, "His bride has made herself ready; it was granted her to clothe herself with fine linen, bright and pure—for the fine linen is the righteous deeds of the saints." Notice the language used here, where it may again spark the debate of whether it is God's grace or our deeds that make us ready. Yet the message is clear; God's grace has made it possible for us to have good deeds through faith and the help of the Holy Spirit (we were *given* the fine linen), but we have to make ourselves (i.e., the Church) ready by putting it on.

This observation underscores, once again, that while good deeds are not how we obtain salvation, they are important, and their significance is made all the more evident during the eschaton. This is because the good deeds of the entire community, the bride, are made up of the good deeds of individual saints. In addition, Rev. 20:12–13 tells us that aside from the book of life, books recording everyone's deeds during their time on earth will also be opened during the final judgment. This means that regardless of whether our names are recorded in the book of life, God has a record of everything we have done during our time on earth, and we will be judged by our deeds.

Indeed, the notion that each will be repaid according to their deeds is something that is repeated in both the Old and New Testament (Ps. 62:12; Prov. 24:12; Matt. 12:36; 16:27; Rom. 2:6; 2 Cor. 5:10; 2 Tim. 4:14). Therefore it is not something that can be dismissed. God has always cared about our deeds. Do we know precisely how God will repay each of us according to our deeds? Unfortunately, we do not, for it is not clearly specified. We only know that our God is a just God; those whose names are in the book of life will be granted eternal life, and God will recompense us based on our deeds. But the important takeaway is that how we live matters, and our faith and actions are something that cannot be uncoupled. Our actions reveal our deeply held beliefs, whether we acknowledge it or not. Thus if we have truly placed our faith in God and remain in Him, it will show. Our faith will naturally be manifested as fruit—deeds that reflect our renewed relationship with God and our identity as members of God's kingdom. James reiterates this point by stating that faith without works is dead (James 2:17).

So how should we live as a community so that we are ready as the holy and blameless bride when Jesus returns? Clearly, a part of it involves each of us trying our best to remain in Christ to live a life pleasing to Him. But being a holy and blameless community is more than just a collection of saintly individuals. The Church as a whole must recognize God's call for us to be holy and blameless, as we strive to be united and live out the Church's role as the physical representation of God and His message of salvation during the "already but not yet" interim. It is recognizing that this is a role that requires our communal prayers and determined focus, acknowledging that this objective should be our top priority because this is how we will be ready for Jesus's return, which is happening at a time no one knows.

Consequently, we strive to love and bear with one another, forgiving each other with the love of Jesus. We serve one another and build up the Church of God. We seek the guidance of the Holy Spirit so as to understand God's word and live out His truth, encouraging each other to follow Jesus. Importantly, we must remind each other to stop sinning and repent before the Lord. Jesus has warned that at the end time, "many will turn away from the faith and will betray and hate each other." There will be false prophets, and "the love of most will grow cold" (Matt. 24:10–12). Is it any surprise that the first part of Revelation contains letters to the

8. THE BRIDE AWAITING HER GROOM

seven churches in Rev. 2:1—3:22, where Jesus repeatedly asked the churches, i.e., the believers, to repent?[2] When Jesus's return is fast approaching, when God will repay us according to our deeds, and the Church is meant to be a holy and blameless bride, of course we must seize the moment and repent and return to God.

So how can we live out God's plan for His Church during the "already but not yet" interim? The above discussion shows us that it is only when (i) we each strive to abide in Jesus, growing deeper in our personal relationship with God; *and* (ii) we also look out for the interests and well-being of everyone in God's community, helping those who are weak, that *together* we can be the light and salt of the world to proclaim the good news of Jesus Christ. This is why we must each take up our role *now*, and strive to be united as faithful witnesses before Jesus's return.

In anticipation of Jesus's return—awaiting the celebration!

Despite the many aspects we have discussed, we are not done with the marriage analogy of God's relationship with His people. What the marriage analogy also illustrates is that when Jesus returns, there will be a celebration and a wedding feast! After all, what is more exciting than the wedding day for those who are engaged? We see in Rev. 19:7 that it will be a joyous celebration, where a great multitude in the heavens will shout, "Let us rejoice and be glad and give him glory! For the wedding of the Lamb has come, and His bride has made herself ready." Indeed, "blessed are those who are invited to the wedding supper of the Lamb" (Rev. 19:9), because those are the ones who have overcome by remaining faithful until the end during the engagement period, thereby evading the second death.

The "already but not yet" is finally over. Jesus has won the final victory against the devil, and He has put an end to all evil and pain. God's people will finally be resurrected, with their bodies transformed, to enter into eternal union with their long-awaited groom Jesus Christ, where they will enjoy worshipping God and fellowshipping with Him in the new heaven and new earth. They will get to witness the full reveal of God's glory, with the new

Jerusalem coming down from heaven, decorated with precious stones and streets of gold. They are the ones who will reign with Christ (Phil. 3:21; Rev. 21:1–8; 22:3–5). There is so much to celebrate; the victory is certain, and our future in eternity is full of all things glorious, majestic, and beautiful beyond our imagination. It will be filled with love, joy, peace, and righteousness because we will see the face of God.

Yet, for many of us, our minds are seemingly consumed by everything that happens *before* the victory and the celebration. Our minds are focused on the signs of the end time, the wars and persecutions, and natural disasters that Jesus warned us about before His departure (Matt. 24:6–9). Sometimes we are fixated on the horrifying images of the apocalypse that are depicted countless times in movies and popular culture. We are concerned with evading the lake of burning sulfur, which is a perfectly justified concern, yet, we have not put much thought into the glorious and marvelous eternity that will come *after* the final judgment. It is like Jesus's disciples, who were understandably grieved to hear Jesus's announcement of His impending death, but were seemingly unable to register the good news of His resurrection three days after the dreaded "end." In a way, our focus on the suffering and fear associated with the end time is completely understandable. This is because the celebration is in the future, pertaining to a realm that is unseen with our eyes right now, but the possibility of having to endure the disasters of the end time is unsettling and frightening.

Nonetheless, we must not let anxiety and fear blind us from the glorious end of God's plan of salvation. Focusing on the celebration of God's eternal reign that will undoubtedly come is important, because it gives us hope when we are still mired in darkness in the "already but not yet." We are sojourners, not just because our time on earth is brief compared to eternity, but because we recognize that earth is not our home. Indeed, we are *not* meant to feel completely at home during our earthly existence, because we belong to Christ, and our values will inevitably clash with that of this world if we follow Jesus. There will be persecutions and sacrifices to make in order to remain faithful to God.

8. THE BRIDE AWAITING HER GROOM

Yet we are not alone in our struggles, because we are sojourners together with other believers. We can encourage each other to hope, focusing on things unseen with our eyes but are certainly coming true in the future, like the long list of God's chosen ones documented in Hebrews 11. They chose to follow God by faith, trusting in Him even if it meant they would be foreigners and sojourners on earth. "They were longing for a better country—a heavenly one. Therefore God is not ashamed to be called their God, for He has prepared a city for them" (Heb. 11:16). When we remember that all suffering is temporary and God's victory and reign is certain, when we remember that we are surrounded by a great cloud of witnesses who chose and are choosing to place their faith in Jesus, we will be able to hang onto the hope and peace that come from Jesus even when things get difficult on earth. As Paul says, "I consider that our present sufferings are not worth comparing with the glory that will be revealed in us" (Rom. 8:18).

Indeed, when our hope is in the eternal reign of God and the new heaven and new earth, then we would not just idly wait for Jesus's return. Instead, we would *longingly anticipate* His second coming. Paul aptly describes this anticipation as an eager expectation in Rom. 8:19–23, as the whole creation groans in the pains of childbirth, waiting to be liberated from the bondage of decay because it is part of the fallen world. We, too, are groaning as we wait for the redemption of our bodies. The groaning described here is an eagerness, because during the "already but not yet," we are trapped in pain and suffering, all of which will go away when Jesus returns. Therefore it is not just an exasperation, but a hopeful and eager longing, where we will actively be on the lookout for Jesus's second coming, because this groaning is only the prelude to the victory and celebration that will come when all creation is made new.

This again echoes the imagery presented by the marriage analogy. In Jewish tradition, when it is time for the wedding feast, the groom will arrive with his wedding party at a time not clearly specified, but often around midnight, to knock on the door of his bride. This is the picture depicted in Jesus's parable of the ten virgins (Matt. 25:5–6). The bride, eager for the groom's arrival, will be on the lookout for his arrival by *being ready*. Very much like Jesus's parable, she would be ready with lamps and jars of oil, because she cannot bear missing the moment of her groom's arrival.

Do we look forward to the arrival of our groom Jesus Christ? Or are we too engrossed with our earthly lives to even think about His second coming? More importantly, are we ready for His return? The Bible is interestingly vague about the timing of Jesus's return. On the one hand, Jesus has made plain the signs of the end time, using the fig tree as an example to tell His disciples that by these signs, they will know that the end is near (Matt. 24:32–33). Yet, on the other hand, the exact day and hour will remain unknown (Matt. 24:36). So, does Jesus want us to know or not to know? I think the answer lies in Jesus's command for His disciples regarding the end time: "Therefore keep watch" (Matt. 24:42). When we see the signs of the end time, we know that time is running out. It serves as a wake-up call for us to seize the moment, whether it is to repent, preach the gospel, love one another, encourage each other, or not lose hope. But when the exact time is unknown, we also will not be able to wait until the exact moment to pledge our faith in Jesus, thereby cheating the system. What Jesus wants from us has been the same all along—we are to *continue to be alert*, trying to live out our calling as individuals and as a community, because this is how we anticipate Jesus's return, this is how we get ready.

Points for Reflection

1. In the realm unseen with our eyes, our God is seated on the throne and reigning right now, glorious and victorious. Does this change the way you view your daily struggles with sins? What are some of the ways your perspective has changed?

8. THE BRIDE AWAITING HER GROOM

2. Revelation shows us that during the "already but not yet" interim, we are in the midst of war, where the devil is constantly looking to lure us away from faithfully following Jesus before Jesus's return. Is this surprising or alarming to you? How does this affect the way you approach your relationship with God?
3. The Church, not individuals, is to be the bride of the Lamb that is holy and blameless when Jesus returns at the end time. Does this realization impact your understanding of God's ultimate will for His people? Is there anything you would do differently regarding your relationship with other believers in light of this realization?

9. APPLICATION: KEEPING THE END IN MIND

LIVING AS A COMMUNITY WITH AN ESCHATOLOGICAL MINDSET

Reflection Question

1. Does knowledge regarding the end time and eternity impact how you live your life now? If yes, how does it affect your walk with God? If not, why not?

Despite everything we have learned about the end time up to this point, the call to live with an eschatological mindset is often difficult to apply because it feels so far away. Nonetheless, the notion that we still have time is one of the biggest lies Satan has successfully put in our hearts. We are fascinated by the symbols and imageries in Revelation, yet what is often overlooked is the message of urgency. This message reminds us that the end time is coming sooner than we think. In fact, Revelation is bookended by this message. In John's

9. APPLICATION: KEEPING THE END IN MIND

introduction of the book, it says, "Blessed is the one who reads aloud the words of this prophecy, and blessed are those who hear it and take to heart what is written in it, because *the time is near*" (Rev. 1:3). The book ends with these verses, "He who testifies to these things says, 'Yes, *I am coming soon.*' Amen. Come, Lord Jesus. The grace of the Lord Jesus be with God's people. Amen" (Rev. 22:20–21).

Jesus is coming soon, very soon. He is telling us to act now, not later; to repent now, not later; to live a Spirit-led life now, not later. Indeed, this is the very mindset evident in multiple epistles in the New Testament. We have Paul, James, Peter, John, and the writer of Hebrews all reminding us that the time is near (Rom. 13:11–12; Heb. 10:25; James 5:8; 1 Pet. 4:7; Rev. 1:3). They are reminding us that since Jesus is coming back very soon, let us rearrange our priorities and choose to live a life pleasing to God, because time is running out. Living with the end time in mind is thus critical in helping us live a Spirit-led life. In this chapter, we will discuss how an eschatological mindset should shape our walk with God as individuals and as a community.

The clocks are ticking—we need to maintain this awareness

Some might say, "The Bible was written almost 2,000 years ago, yet Jesus has not returned. Is He truly coming back soon like He said He would?" Indeed, generations of believers have passed away without seeing this promise come true. But a similar question has already been asked back in the first century (2 Pet. 3:4), and here is how Peter the Apostle addresses the query. First, he points out that we as creatures are in no place to doubt the plan of the Creator, because by the word of God, the heaven and earth were created, and "by the same word the present heavens and earth are reserved for fire, being kept for the day of judgment and destruction of the ungodly" (2 Pet. 3:7). Jesus is definitely coming back, even if it has not happened yet.

Second, Peter urges us to remember that "with the Lord a day is like a thousand years, and a thousand years are like a day . . . The day of the Lord will come like a thief. The heavens will disappear with a roar; the elements will be destroyed by fire, and the earth and everything done in it will be laid bare" (2 Pet. 3:8, 10). Peter is referring to the fact that our God and His ways are completely beyond our grasp and control. There is no way for us creatures to know or even guess the timing of His return, nor can we prepare for this critical moment with our earthly ways. When He comes, everything will happen so quickly and unexpectedly that we will not be able to maneuver or control the situation in any way. It will be too late to run, to scuffle, to remedy. We will not have enough time to get ready. This is why Jesus urged us to *get ready now*, when everything looks perfectly fine, and it seems like there is still plenty of time, or we will never be ready. The clock is ticking, even if we do not see or acknowledge it.

But this is not the only clock that is ticking. Yes, the "already but not yet" interim is the time for humans to respond to God's call to repent and follow Him. Nonetheless, as discussed previously, each of us only has our time on earth to respond by choosing to accept the gift of salvation and to live accordingly. Once our time on earth is up, it will be too late.[1] The urgency is heightened when we think about the transient nature of our existence. We are like grass, a mist that will appear for a little while before it vanishes (Isa. 40:6–8; James 4:14).

None of us know when our time on earth will abruptly come to an end. This is a truth that we are all aware of, yet we leave it locked up in the corner of our minds most of the time. We are only forced to come to terms with this harsh reality when natural disasters strike, or in the face of diseases or accidents, when we acknowledge with a newfound humility the frailty of human existence, and how little control we have over the length of our own lives. So many of us live like the rich fool in Jesus's parable, who thought that he could "take life easy; eat, drink and be merry" because his land has yielded an abundant harvest. What he did not know was that his life would be demanded from him that night (Luke 12:16–20).

Living with an eschatological mindset is thus recognizing that both clocks are ticking, and irrespective of whether our time is up

9. APPLICATION: KEEPING THE END IN MIND

because our lives have come to an end or because Jesus has returned, we must maintain this sense of urgency in our daily life. It is recognizing each day given to us as a gift and an opportunity to respond to God with our lives, instead of taking it for granted. Time is running out, and the end is certain. What will our response be?

Still, the above discussion is not new for most people. If the scripture has repeatedly warned us of the urgency of the situation, why have we not responded? One possibility is that some of us subconsciously think that, unlike what the Bible describes (Matt. 24:37–41), we will still have a little time to get ready when the moment hits. After all, the absoluteness of God's timing and His authority is something we are not used to in today's society, because we are never short on resources to help us get things done, or get away with things.

But if we think we will be able to "get ready" by taking our faith seriously only in the final moments, we are missing the point. First, God our Creator has absolute authority over the timing of the eschaton and the ending of all creation, including ourselves, upon Jesus's return. He is a righteous God who cannot be fooled. Second, salvation is not about sneaking into heaven, but it is about accepting God's amazing gift and living as God's witnesses and members of His kingdom. It was never Jesus's intention to only get us into heaven; His plan is for us to be *ready now* because our lives are already transformed by abiding in Him while we are still here. Getting ready is a continuous state, not a moment to be caught. May we learn to fear God and live with His wisdom even though our days on earth are short.

Run the race—resetting our priorities

When we recognize that our days on earth are short and our time is limited, then we need to acknowledge that living with an eschatological mindset also means resetting our priorities. Sadly, many of us have been living without examining our priorities in life and how we should spend our time. Have you ever been asked this question, "If you know that you only have one month to live, how would you live differently?" What this question and its answers reveal is the fact that a lot of time, we are not living in accordance with what we think is truly important in life. More often than not, we are just going with the flow, or we live with the assumption that we will always have time to finally get to the things that truly matter. Sometimes we also feel like we cannot afford to live according to our priorities because our demanding lives have left us no breathing space. But this would mean that we have somehow let the world's values or unexamined habits determine how we spend our time, as we roam purposelessly with our lives.

But Eph. 5:15–17 (ESV) says, "Look carefully then how you walk, not as unwise but as wise, making the best use of the time, because the days are evil. Therefore do not be foolish, but understand what the will of the Lord is." Paul is precisely reminding us that because time is limited, *think carefully* about how you spend your time, using it to walk in the way of the Lord. We need to focus, like those who are running in a race to win a prize, because "we do it to get a crown that will last forever" (1 Cor. 9:25). We must stop letting ourselves be distracted and occupied by worries of this life and chasing after things that have little eternal values, because Jesus's return can happen anytime. John reminds us, "Do not love the world or anything in the world. If anyone loves the world, love for the Father is not in them" (1 John 2:15). This is not a verse to tell us that we should ignore our life on earth, but it is about our hearts, about what we adore and worship. We keep thinking that we can do both, to love this world a little and God a little. But here we are reminded that we are only capable of worshipping the world *or* our God. Therefore we need to focus and keep our eyes on the prize.

So what exactly are the things worthy of our time while we are still here? First, if any of us have yet to accept Christ as Savior, we must seize our moment on earth to accept this gift of salvation through faith that will grant us eternal life instead of eternal destruction. Second, if salvation is eternal life in the new heaven and new earth where we will be united with our God forever, then we must focus on our relationship with God because this is what we will have for eternity. We must therefore form the habit of being in

9. APPLICATION: KEEPING THE END IN MIND

the presence of God through His words and through prayers, so that we will know who our God is and who we are. By remaining in His love, we will learn to fellowship with Him, worship Him, rest in Him, and experience the joy and fulfillment that comes with being joined to our Creator.

Third, because we have received God's love and mercy and also because He is a righteous God who will repay each of us according to our deeds, we aim to rely on the Holy Spirit to help us live in a way that is pleasing to Him one day at a time. We repent and put off the sins that so easily entangle and strive to be faithful witnesses of God's love, mercy, and justice in our lives, bringing the good news to those around us. We focus on building up the body of Christ and loving one another in the Church of God, so that we can stand firm together as one until the end. While this does not mean that all of us should quit our jobs and serve God full time, it does remind us that whatever we do, we "do it all for the glory of God" (1 Cor. 10:31). Do it for His kingdom, and for the people that He loves. We are only asked to be faithful in running the race He calls us to run.

Does the above sound just like the usual teaching for Christian living? Yes, it does. What the eschatological mindset brings is not a different set of criteria regarding how we should live as children of God. The difference lies in our attitude toward these teachings. Paul explains this critical change in our attitude in Rom. 13:11–12. "And do this, understanding the present time: The hour has already come for you to wake up from your slumber, because our salvation is nearer now than when we first believed. The night is nearly over; the day is almost here. So let us put aside the deeds of darkness and put on the armor of light." Here is how Peter encourages believers to stay alert, "The end of all things is near. Therefore be alert and of sober mind so that you may pray" (1 Pet. 4:7).

The end is coming and we are running out of time. If these are the essential things, why are they constantly being put off? Will we wait idly around if we know an explosion is about to happen? Wouldn't we grab our most precious possessions and say our last words to loved ones before it is too late? Precisely because time is running out, let us choose to seek Him first and do what is right before the Lord, even if it is difficult. Let us choose to love one another and seek peace and unity within the Church, even if it appears futile. The eschatological mindset gives us a reason to be focused and determined, because time is running out.

The earth is not heaven—persevere in anticipation of Jesus's return

Maybe at this point, some of us will share that we have indeed tried our best to honor God in everything we do, because we *are* aware that we are each given only a finite amount of time to serve God. Yet, regardless of how determined we might be, things could get difficult, or the outcome could be disheartening. There are also days when we truly struggle to remain focused on God when life gets demanding. Our journey to follow God is seemingly full of good intentions and the most earnest effort, but peace and joy are not always the outcome. The frustration can be very real.

But this is when we need to realize that while we are called to follow God and live out our identity as members of God's kingdom, we are still in a fallen world. As discussed, tribulation and the clash of God's kingdom with the world will only worsen as Jesus's return draws near. The devil is actively wreaking havoc to lead us away from God. Thus as much as we are called to be a channel of God's love, mercy, and justice during our time here, and to be faithful witnesses of God and His plan of salvation, *the earth is not heaven*. This means that despite our best effort, things may not have the happy endings we had hoped for, and there will still be disappointments, misery, and pain until Jesus returns to wipe away all tears.

How, then, should we handle the frustration as we await Jesus's return? First, it is essential to remember that regardless of how things look, God is in control, and He has a plan. His ways are higher than our ways, and He is the God who can turn all situations into blessings. Rom. 8:28 says, "And we know that in all things God works for the good of those who love him, who have been

9. APPLICATION: KEEPING THE END IN MIND

called according to his purpose." It reminds us to look away from our situations and look to God, whose definition of good may not be the same as ours, but we can trust Him because He alone knows what is truly good for us as our Creator and Savior.

In addition, it is important to acknowledge that the good or benefits God intends for His people are often beyond our individual, personal benefits, nor are the benefits necessarily evident immediately. Instead, sometimes we only see the benefits in the long run, and when we look at it from the community and kingdom perspective. For example, when Stephen from the early church was martyred, it was definitely a loss when we look at it from Stephen's personal perspective and for those who loved him. Yet, it led to the rapid spread of the gospel to the neighboring regions (Acts 7:54—8:4). The earth is indeed not heaven, but our God reigns, and He is in control. We have to trust in His wisdom, His ways, and His timing.

Second, we need to recognize that we are never supposed to have all the happy endings on earth. God, in His grace, has granted us many blessings while we are still here, but earth is never meant to take the place of our eternal home. We are sojourners; our experience on earth or our perception of it is but a small fraction of our existence compared to the life we will have in eternity. We must remember that in the realm unseen, our God, who is seated on the throne, is keeping a record of every act we have done, including those done out of love for God and others. He sees every attempt to honor Him in our lives, He knows all the good intentions and earnest effort we have put in, and He will reward us, even if these efforts do not achieve what we think they should achieve on earth. This is the hope we can hang on to, the hope that our righteous God will see our hearts and efforts. "Therefore, my dear brothers and sisters, stand firm. Let nothing move you. Always give yourselves fully to the work of the Lord, because you know that your labor in the Lord is not in vain" (1 Cor. 15:58).

More importantly, when we recognize that the earth is not heaven, it gives us a reason to long for Jesus's return, to long for the home that will truly be ours. It reminds us to live expectantly, to anticipate patiently for the true reward of our faith. In Paul's letters to the Corinthians, here is how he encourages his fellow believers. "Therefore we do not lose heart. Though outwardly we are wasting away, yet inwardly we are being renewed day by day. For our light and momentary troubles are achieving for us an eternal glory that far outweighs them all. So we fix our eyes not on what is seen, but on what is unseen, since what is seen is temporary, but what is unseen is eternal" (2 Cor. 4:16–18). Our suffering is temporary and sometimes inevitable as a member of God's kingdom in this fallen world. But as we share in Jesus's suffering, we, too, will one day share in His glory, so long as we continue to stand firm in the Lord and don't lose heart.

Third, because we have our eternal home and future glory to look forward to, we must learn to persevere patiently when we wait for Jesus's return. In today's world, where we are used to efficiency and fast results, patience and perseverance are almost like lost arts in our society. But this is precisely why we need to make a conscious effort to be patient and not give up during this process. To do this, we must put on the full armor of God and pray incessantly for each other in God's community. Paul describes the armor of God as including the belt of truth, the breastplate of righteousness, a readiness of our feet that comes from the gospel of peace, the shield of faith, the helmet of salvation, and the word of God as a sword (Eph. 6:14–17). Notice how every piece of armor is a gift from God. What we need to do is simply put them on and hang on tightly to our sword, so that we can stand firm against the devil's scheme.

Indeed, there is no standing firm unless we remain rooted in God and His love. But to continue persevering, especially in the face of repeated tribulations and disappointments, we also need prayers and support from our brothers and sisters. "And pray in the Spirit on all occasions with all kinds of prayers and requests. With this in mind, be alert and always keep on praying for all the Lord's people" (Eph. 6:18). Everyone will be downhearted sometimes, regardless of how strong or determined we are. This is why we must find in our community those we can journey together, someone with whom we can lift each other up in prayers and encouragement, while also

9. APPLICATION: KEEPING THE END IN MIND

keeping each other accountable on this journey. We need companions whose hearts are in the Lord so that we will be encouraged to keep persevering until the end.

Then, maybe after we have hung on together and helped each other through all the ups and downs during this interim, we can each say with confidence:

> *I have fought the good fight, I have finished the race, I have kept the faith. Now there is in store for me the crown of righteousness, which the Lord, the righteous Judge, will award to me on that day—and not only to me, but also to all who have longed for his appearing.*
>
> 2 Timothy 4:7–8

Points for Reflection

1. One of the key messages in Revelation is the message of urgency. How does this sense of urgency affect your priorities in life? Are you aware of how you have been spending your time?
2. What are the hurdles preventing you from getting ready for Jesus's return? Pray and ask God to reveal them to you, write them down in your journal, and ask for His strength and grace to help you maintain the focus on Him.
3. Does the idea that we are sojourners on earth give you peace? If yes, why? If not, why not? In your prayer, ask God to open your eyes so that you will see the hope and comfort that come with the promise of Jesus's return.

SPECIAL TOPIC: PREDESTINATION
DOES PREDESTINATION MEAN THAT OUR FAITH AND DEEDS ARE UNIMPORTANT?

"If every person who is saved has been predestined for salvation by God before we came into the world, then what is the significance of the personal choice we make to accept Christ?"

"Does it still matter how we live our lives during the 'already but not yet' interim?"

One theological concept we have yet to discuss but is intricately linked to our salvation is the notion of predestination. While the point here is not to delve into the centuries of debate on this topic, certain clarification is needed in light of our discussion of the eschaton and the ends we each face when Jesus returns. Predestination is the notion that everyone who is saved has been pre-determined by God, meaning those who will eventually accept the gift of salvation were chosen by God before the foundation of the world. Eph. 1:4 says, "For He chose us in Him before the Creation of the world to be holy and blameless in His sight." Rev. 13:8 echoes this concept, revealing that those whose names are

SPECIAL TOPIC: PREDESTINATION

in the book of life have been written since the foundation of the world.

Understandably, this concept raises several questions regarding the mechanism of salvation, and it seemingly contradicts what we know so far regarding how anyone comes to accept Christ. In particular, if every person who is saved has been predestined for salvation by God before we came into the world, then what is the significance of the personal choice we make to accept Christ? In addition, if we have been predestined to receive eternal life when Jesus returns, does it still matter how we live our lives during the "already but not yet" interim? Another question many would have is, why would God choose only to predestine certain people for salvation, and more importantly, am I one of the chosen ones?

These questions are completely reasonable. But before we try to answer any of them, we need to acknowledge that we, as creatures, are not supposed to know the answer to every question. As discussed earlier, our God is the Creator and we are His creatures; it is not in our nature to fully comprehend God's being and His will. We only know as much as God has chosen in His will and sovereignty to reveal to us; beyond that, many things will remain a mystery. For example, of the questions raised, what will always remain a mystery to us is why God has decided to predestine only certain people, and not everyone, for eternal life. There are various discussions as to why this may be the case, but since the Bible is not explicit about it, we need to recognize that we will likely not have a definitive answer.

The other question we will never have the answer to is whether I or the person next to me is one of the chosen ones. None of us will know whose names are written in the book of life until that day when we each stand before the judgment seat of God. We are not privy to this information; it is not the will of God that we know the answers to these questions. Yet God has not kept the notion of predestination a complete secret. It is His will that we are informed that for those of us who are saved, we have been predestined. Thus before we address the other questions raised regarding predestination, a more important question we should ask, is what is God trying to tell us by revealing to us that we are predestined?

Rom. 8:29–30 contains the most well-known verses regarding the concept of predestination. "For those God foreknew He also predestined to be conformed to the image of His Son, that He might be the firstborn among many brothers and sisters. And those He predestined, He also called; those He called, He also justified; those He justified, He also glorified." Notice that these two verses cover the entire journey of our salvation, from when we were predestined for salvation, to when we are called to repent and accept this gift of salvation, to when we are justified by the blood of Jesus when we call Him our Savior, and finally, to when we will be glorified together with Jesus when He returns.

The most important revelation from this passage is the fact that God, *not us*, is the one who initiates and eventually fulfills our salvation. Yes, each of us has personally gone through the process of getting to know about Jesus and the good news; each of us has made the decision to accept Christ as our Savior. But this passage reveals that none of us would even be receptive to the gospel in the first place if not for the predestination of God. He has been calling us, guiding us, and eventually enabling us to accept this good news. This means that for those of us who have accepted this gift of salvation, we really have nothing to boast about. We are not better than those who refuse to accept Christ because we chose correctly or wisely. The only thing that sets us apart from non-believers is God's predestination. True, it is something we do not completely understand, but the significance of this concept for our faith is to help us recognize that there is no room for any pride and self-righteousness regarding our salvation. It is and always will be a complete gift of God's mercy and grace, and our only logical response is gratitude. This is one of the essential messages we must garner from the concept of predestination.

Second, we notice from v.29 that those who are predestined are predestined to *be conformed to the image of Jesus*. This again reminds us that our deeds are supposed to express our faith. We have thought for so long that we are saved by faith alone that our actions do not matter. But the scripture has made it clear that the two are never uncoupled from each other. Our relationship with God is restored

SPECIAL TOPIC: PREDESTINATION

by faith and faith alone; but because of our restored relationship with God, our deeds will change accordingly to reflect this faith when we continue to abide in Jesus.

Yet what the notion of predestination conveys is a message of *assurance and comfort*. Phil. 1:6 (ESV) says, "And I am sure of this, that He who began a good work in you will bring it to completion at the day of Jesus Christ." When God reminds us that we have been predestined and that He Himself will bring our salvation to fruition at the very end, He is reminding us that we can trust Him with our eternal destiny. We can rest in the Lord, knowing that even with the ups and downs in our journey with Him, He will carry us through to the end. We can rest in His love knowing that our salvation is secure because it has been in His hand this whole time. We do not need to run ourselves dry to ensure our own salvation, because those God predestined, He will eventually glorify.

Thus, with the notion of predestination, God has granted us two important revelations even if we do not fully comprehend this concept. First, we must recognize that salvation is a complete gift; none of us can boast about our salvation even though we each made the personal choice to accept Christ as our Savior. Second, the notion of predestination gives us assurance that God, who started the good work, will carry us through to the end. God knows our hearts and whether we have continually acknowledged Him as our Lord and Savior. He knows whether our faith is in Him. We can trust in His love and faithfulness.

SO HOW DO these revelations affect our daily walk with God? We are now ready to return to two of the questions raised earlier in this section, namely, what is the significance of the personal choice we make to accept Christ, and whether the way we live our lives during our time on earth matters. The questions are concerned with two particular stages in our Christian walk. The first question concerns our role in becoming a believer. The notion of predestination may indeed make it sound like the importance of our personal choice has been minimized. But this is when we need to be reminded that we will never know the identity of those predestined for salvation. This means that for us, the choices that are laid out before us are identical with or without the knowledge of whether we have been predestined—we can choose to accept this gift of salvation or not.[1] While God may know who will eventually become a believer, we don't. Therefore, it is still our responsibility to accept this gift of salvation, thereby bearing our responsibility of responding to God's call.

Likewise, it is pointless to wonder if we should preach the gospel to those around us just in case they have not been predestined. It is something neither we nor they will know. Therefore we preach the gospel all the same, and each of those who have heard the good news will have the responsibility to choose to respond or not respond to God's invitation on a personal level. When the end time comes, we might look back and realize that some of us were never destined for salvation; but that knowledge will come later, not now. For each of us, the choices have been given to us *now*, and our responsibility is to respond *now*.

As for those who have already made the decision to accept Jesus as Savior, the second question concerns whether the way we live our lives, as in our deeds, matters if we have been predestined to be conformed to the image of Jesus. A simple answer would be yes, because if predestination does not remove our responsibility in accepting Jesus as our Savior, it also does not excuse us from living a life that honors our restored relationship with God. Predestination is not a justification that allows us to skip over all our responsibility in our relationship with God. But a more thorough answer would require us to revisit what we mean when we ask if our deeds "matter." Do deeds matter, as in whether we will be saved because of our deeds? This we already know the answer to; we can never save ourselves *by our deeds*. And yet our deeds matter because God has chosen us to be holy and blameless in His sight, so that our deeds reflect not only our restored relationship with God, but also our identity as members of God's kingdom.

It is about the motives that are hidden in our hearts. If our daily choice of following the Spirit through our deeds is done with the

SPECIAL TOPIC: PREDESTINATION

motive of securing salvation, this is a futile attempt, because the notion of predestination reminds us that salvation is a gift. But when our attempts to live in a way that is pleasing to God are made as a response to God's love, God's predestination brings new significance to our faith. It grants us the comfort and assurance in knowing that even when we occasionally succumb to sins and have our moments of doubt, God will bring our salvation to fruition in the end because He is faithful. For those God has chosen, He has promised to send the Holy Spirit to help us be conformed to the image of Jesus. Indeed, when our relationship with God is the reality that we experience daily, when we continually return to God to seek Him regardless of how we have been and experience His love and guidance, there is really no need for us to wonder if we are predestined anymore. We can rest in His love knowing that He will surely transform us, guide us, and be with us forever in the new heaven and new earth.

CONCLUSION: LEANING ON GOD AS HIS BELOVED

We are at the end of our discussion. Many topics and concepts related to our salvation, our spiritual journey, and how we should relate to God and others have been discussed. We see that our restored relationship with God is not merely about the individual and personal aspect of our faith, but it is related to our relationship with others inside and outside of the Church. It grants us the context to comprehend many of the Bible's teachings in every phase and aspect of our spiritual journey, allowing us to piece together seemingly disjointed teachings. Indeed, the aim of the book is to help us apply various teachings and theological concepts to our daily walk with God, because our God is alive and He is at work in every area of our lives. What we learn from the Bible or theology books is thus not simply a set of rules and theories in our heads. They are meaningful, significant, and applicable to every believer's life, so we can "test and approve what God's will is—His good, pleasing and perfect will" (Rom. 12:2).

CONCLUSION: LEANING ON GOD AS HIS BELOVED

Applying these reminders to our individual walk with God

Nonetheless, since no two of our personal journeys with God are the same, nor are we all at the same place in our journeys, the specific areas of growth, and the direction and extent of growth in relation to the topics discussed could be very different for each of us. In our discussion, generalizations are sometimes necessary to address believers from various phases of the spiritual journey, but what we each need to focus on differs. For example, the reminder to be rooted in the transforming love of God could mean very different things for different believers. For those who are somewhat burnout in our effort to love and serve God, this is a reminder to examine if we have been serving with our own strength, or if we have been serving out of insecurities. It reminds us to return to the love of God and know that there is no need for us to earn His love through work and services, because we are worthy and loved as is. But for those whose faith has remained as head knowledge, to be rooted in the transforming love of God means responding to God's call to be transformed and start living for God. It is realizing that with the help of the Holy Spirit, we can indeed live differently, because we have been released from the bondage of sin by the blood of Jesus. This is illustrated in Figure 1.

But how do we know where we are on the arbitrary spectrum shown in Figure 1? The only way to know is to quiet down before God and prayerfully reflect on our daily walk with Him. As we form the habit of reflecting on our lives and asking the Holy Spirit to reveal our sins and areas of growth, we will not only grow more familiar with the voice and guidance of the Holy Spirit, but we will become more aware of our inner state. In God's grace and love, we will be able to come face to face with our sins, struggles, fears, and exhaustion, some of which are hidden deep inside us, and seek His help with them. This is the awareness that prompts us to repent and seek forgiveness. It is also how we will learn to eventually surrender our entire being to Him—our will, our reason, and our emotions, so that we can live an increasingly God-centered life.

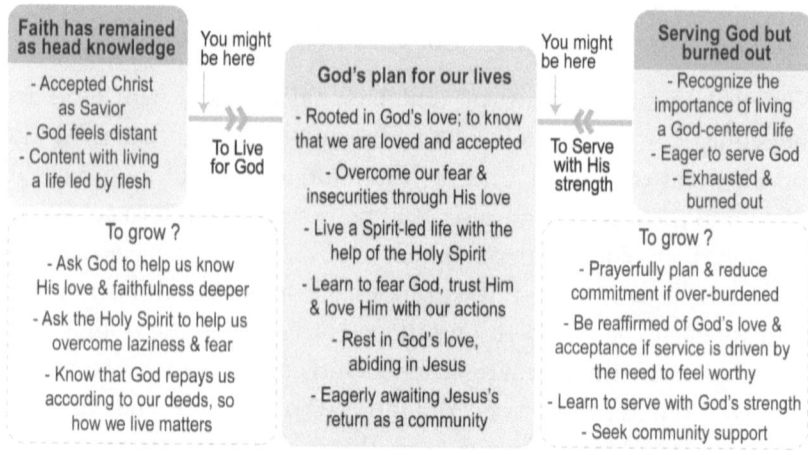

Figure 1. Imagine if we can establish a spectrum of "living a God-centered life with His strength," we will notice that at the ends of the spectrum are two possible situations from which we can grow toward the midpoint. The midpoint represents the state we are supposed to be in when we abide in Jesus and rest in His love. The lessons we each should learn depends on where we are on this spectrum.

An overarching theme: we can never be, nor are we supposed to be, independent from God

Nonetheless, the above diagram only shows one of the many spectrums we fall on in our walk with God. We can draw many more of these spectrums. Figure 2 shows us what some of them may look like. These spectrums collectively represent our journey when we try to live a life pleasing to God—because as we grow in our knowledge of God and ourselves and mature in our faith, our positions along every spectrum shift. For example, we may initially think of God mostly as a stern God because of His justice, so we respond well to teaching about fearing Him, but we have a hard time trusting in His love and kindness. Yet as we continue to journey with God, we will slowly come to understand how He lovingly accepts our entire being and how He is faithful, and we finally know in our hearts and minds that our God is indeed both loving and just. Along every spectrum, we are all growing toward the center, whether in our knowledge or the way we live, to a more balanced

CONCLUSION: LEANING ON GOD AS HIS BELOVED

and accurate understanding of God and our relationship with Him. This, in turn, gives us a clearer picture of how to grow and apply the Bible's teachings in our spiritual journey.

Figure 2. Our spiritual journey is made up of multiple spectrums along which we grow. As we come to know God and ourselves better through God's word and prayerful introspection, the Holy Spirit will reveal areas in our lives that require more of God's transforming love and grace, so that we can live an increasingly God-centered, Spirit-led life.

Still, the above diagram fails to convey an important detail about our spiritual journey. We might picture a maturing faith as us growing steadily toward the center of every spectrum on our journey of sanctification, so that we will finally arrive at the midpoint mark of the spectrums. We might think that once we have learned and attained the secret of this perfect balance, we will remain there, having "conquered" these aspects of our faith. Yet, in reality, not only do we have a hard time determining if the midpoint mark has been reached, but ensuring that we always stay and act from that perfect spot is much harder than we think. Indeed, how many times have we responded to God's call by taking a step to serve Him in church ministry, only to slowly lose the joy of serving Him, and our duty became a burden? We were headed toward the midpoint mark, but before we knew it, we had landed on the other end of the spectrum. Furthermore, we often have a hard time deciding the perfect balance between fearing God and resting in His love, even when we recognize that our God is both loving and just. We do not even know if we are already too individualistic, let alone juggling the balance between the importance of community and our personal faith.

This reality reminds us that despite everything we have learned, there is no guidebook or analysis for us to "hit the mark" on our own. Living a Spirit-led life is not a skill set we can acquire, because it was never God's intention for us to attain this knowledge so that we can proceed to live independently from Him. As creatures, we are not given minds that would have the way of the Lord all understood and deciphered by ourselves, nor can we withstand the devil's scheme to derail us when we are apart from God. We are asked to follow His lead, not walk on our own, because God knows that we will never grasp the sweet spot of acting justly and loving mercy *without walking humbly with Him* (Mic. 6:8). After all, what God has granted us is a restored relationship with Him. What is left of a relationship if we are to sidestep Him after we think we have it all figured out? Rather, the knowledge and insights we have obtained serve to remind us that our understanding of God and His commands is partial and incomplete, and that we are limited and vulnerable. Regardless of how much we have learned and grown, we will always desperately need God.

Therefore, if there is one concluding message from the book, it would be to *lean on God at all times*, and learn to *rest in this dependence*. Everything we have discussed only comes alive when we realize that God is holding our hands to *show* us what His word means and what it is like to walk with Him. He himself will show us how to hit the mark for His glory, and when we fail, we can trust that He does not stop teaching us and forgiving us when we turn back. All we need to do is make up our minds to follow Him and give our best effort to abide in Him, and we will get to witness God's grace and His

CONCLUSION: LEANING ON GOD AS HIS BELOVED

unsurpassable greatness in our inadequacy. We can rest in this relationship with God, patiently trusting in His perfect will and timing, because we know who holds our hands and our future. Maybe with time, we will see that this relationship of dependence and complete reliance, when we honor God for who He is every moment of our lives, is the single most precious thing we will ever experience.

> *But he said to me, "My grace is sufficient for you,*
> *for my power is made perfect in weakness."*
> *Therefore I will boast all the more gladly about my weaknesses, so that Christ's power may rest on me.*
>
> 2 Corinthians 12:9

IN A RELATIONSHIP WITH GOD

A Closing Prayer—10 Daily Reminders

FOLLOWING GOD IS A DAILY CHOICE. Sometimes it is not because we are unwilling; we simply lose focus. So here are ten reminders regarding our Christian walk that will help us remember who God is, who we are, and how we should live for God every day.

1. I am not my own lord; you are. I bear your name, and how I live matters.
2. I am deeply loved and precious in your eyes. I am limited and fragile, but I am in the hand of a God who loves and accepts me.
3. You are a good God who has given me and will give me everything I need.
4. In your love, you have set me free from my sins, my past, and the world's value. So today, in my freedom, I choose to do your will because I love you.
5. I choose to be a channel of your love, goodness, kindness, mercy, and justice to those around me. Teach me how to honor you as the Lord of all my relationships, so that your love and grace will transform my interaction with everybody.
6. You love the Church and everyone who belongs to you. Teach me to love the Church the way you love it. Let me preach the good news; let me focus on building up and edifying brothers and sisters, instead of tearing them down.
7. I will trust in your power, your guidance, your way. Teach me to seek your way and rely on your strength instead of my own.
8. I will not hide from you. When I fail, I will return to you and seek your forgiveness, because you are a faithful God.

CONCLUSION: LEANING ON GOD AS HIS BELOVED

9. I know that whatever comes my way, you have not stopped watching over me and shaping me. Teach me to wait patiently on you and your timing.
10. You are an awesome God. Teach me to be alert and live with the fear of God in my days as a sojourner on earth. Remind me that I have a heavenly home to look forward to, and one day Jesus will return, victorious and glorious.

Ask and it will be given to you; seek and you will find;
knock and the door will be opened to you.
For everyone who asks receives; the one who seeks finds;
and to the one who knocks, the door will be opened.

Matthew 7:7–8

Those whom I love I rebuke and discipline.
So be earnest and repent.
Here I am! I stand at the door and knock.
If anyone hears my voice and opens the door,
I will come in and eat with that person, and they with me.

Revelation 3:19–20

REFERENCES
FOR FURTHER READING

Anderson, Ray S. *On Being Human: Essays in Theological Anthropology*. Eugene: Wipf & Stock Pub, 2010.

Arnold, Clinton. *Ephesians*. Zondervan Exegetical Commentary on the New Testament. Grand Rapids: Zondervan Academic, 2010.

Beasley-Murray, George R. *John*. Word Biblical Commentary Vol. 36. Dallas: Word Books, 1999.

Braaten, Carl E., and Jenson, Robert W. *Christian Dogmatics*, Vol. 2. Philadelphia: Fortress Press, 2011.

Davids, Peter H. *The Letters of 2 Pet.er and Jude*. The Pillar New Testament Commentary. Grand Rapids: William B. Eerdmans, 2006.

Fee, Gordon D. *The First and Second Letters to the Thessalonians*. The New International Commentary on the New Testament. Grand Rapids: William B. Eerdmans, 2009.

Gibbs, Jaffrey. *Matthew 1:1-11:1: A Theological Exposition of Sacred Scripture*. Concordia Commentary. St. Louis: Concordia Publishing, 2006.

Hamilton, Victor P. *The Book of Genesis*. New International Commentary on the Old Testament Series. Chapter 1-17. Grand Rapids: William B. Eerdmans, 1990.

Hansen, G. Walter. *The Letter to the Philippians*. The Pillar New Testament Commentary. Grand Rapids: William B. Eerdmans, 2009.

Jewett, Paul K. *God, Creation, and Revelation: A Neo-Evangelical Theology*. Grand Rapids: William B. Eerdmans, 1991.

Johnson, Darrell. *Discipleship on the Edge: An Expository Journey Through the Book of Revelation*. Vancouver: Regent College Publishing, 2004.

Marshall, I. Howard. *Acts: An Introduction and Commentary*. Tyndale New Testament Commentaries, Vol. 5. Downers Grove: IVP Academic, 2008.

Stott, John R.W. *The Message of Romans: God's Good News for the World (Bible Speaks Today)*. Downers Grove: IVP Academic, 2001.

Webster, John. *Holiness*. Grand Rapids: William B. Eerdmans, 2003.

Zizioulas, John. *Being as Communion: Studies in Personhood and the Church*. New York: St. Vladimir's Seminary Press, 1997.

NOTES

1. Revisiting the Good News

1. Thayer, Greek-English Lexicon of the NT, 21981.
2. The word "work" in Greek can also be translated as "deeds or actions". Friberg, Analytical Greek Lexicon, 11394.

2. God's Original Design

1. The term "The LORD God" is used 19 times in Genesis 2–3 (out of the 37 total incidences in the entire Old Testament).

4. Revelation through Jesus

1. This is not to suggest that all three persons of the Holy Trinity carry out the same tasks. Different aspects of God's work are preeminently associated with different persons of the Trinity—for the Father, it is the task of creation; for the Son, the task of salvation; for the Spirit, the task of sanctification. But none of them complete the task on their own. Instead, they all take part in each task, thus preserving the unity of the triune God.
2. Friberg, Analytical Greek Lexicon, 119; 28048.
3. Friberg, Analytical Greek Lexicon, 5505.

5. Application: Walking with God

1. It is important to note that this verse does not suggest that God's love for people is contingent on our fear of Him. God does *not* only love those who fear Him. What Ps. 103:17-18 emphasizes is how God's love for those in a relationship and a covenant with Him is everlasting. God loves everyone, including those who have not accepted Christ. The invitation to restore their relationship with God stands. But when their relationship is not restored, they will never understand how much God loves them, because this knowledge only comes when we experience it in our relationship with Him.

7. Application: Living as One Community

1. Friberg, Analytical Greek Lexicon, 11442; and Danker, Greek NT Lexicon, 2705.
2. Friberg, Analytical Greek Lexicon, 15900; and Danker, Greek NT Lexicon, 3649.

NOTES

3. Friberg, Analytical Greek Lexicon, 26280; Liddell-Scott, Greek Lexicon (Abridged), 42042; and Danker, Greek NT Lexicon, 6293.
4. The meaning of the verb "accept" according to Friberg, Analytical Greek Lexicon, 23508.
5. Rom. 12:13; the meaning of the noun "hospitality" according to Friberg, Analytical Greek Lexicon, 28087.
6. Friberg, Analytical Greek Lexicon, 2060; Danker, Greek NT Lexicon, 6293.
7. We need to be wise when cultivating in-depth friendships with fellow believers. Beware of inappropriately intimate interactions in the name of fellowship, because it can lead to a lot of temptations and confusion. Above all, pray; and trust that God will bring support and comfort in His ways and timing.

8. The Bride Awaiting Her Groom

1. Gingrich, Greek NT Lexicon, 44.
2. The word "repent" is used eight times in Rev. 2:1—3:22, addressing five of the seven churches, including Ephesus, Pergamum, Thyatira, Sardis, and Laodicea.

9. Application: Keeping the End in Mind

1. It is not the intention here to address the topic of universal salvation or whether people who have never heard the gospel will certainly be denied eternal life. Instead, the focus is to stress our personal responsibility to respond, for all those who have already heard the good news.

Special Topic: Predestination

1. A second debate that stems from the notion of predestination concerns whether humans are indeed given free will, or the extent or nature of the free will that has been given to us. It is not the intention of the current section to go into an in-depth discussion on this topic, but what is important for Christian living is the acknowledgment that God has given us the ability to respond to him through our own choices. The freedom to respond whichever way we want is at the core of the idea of "free will," even if our choices can be influenced by various factors.

ABOUT THE AUTHOR

ZELDA CHEUNG graduated from China Graduate School of Theology, Hong Kong, with a Master of Christian Studies in biblical hermeneutics. A former scientist and teacher, she enjoys studying God's word and hopes that her writing will be a blessing to others. She is now a preacher and Sunday school teacher at the English Congregation of the church she attends.

Visit www.inarelationshipwithgod.com for more of her writing.

www.ingramcontent.com/pod-product-compliance
Lightning Source LLC
Chambersburg PA
CBHW030000110526
44587CB00011BA/923